CLARIBEL COREANO

So, You Want to be a *Life Coach?*

LIFE COACHING GUIDE & WORKBOOK

OFFERING YOU THE TOOLS YOU NEED TO BE EQUIPPED FOR LIFE

EMPOWER
GLOBAL COACHING

ISBN: 978-1-964619-11-8

Dedication

This book is dedicated In Honor of my Father
Eligio Raphael Garcia-Santana.
July 8, 1932-April 29, 2022
Also
For every person who has suffered childhood abuse, neglect,
domestic violence or any other traumatic experiences.
I pray for your healing.

Acknowledgements

With Special Thanks:

First and foremost, I want to give God the glory for allowing me to survive many situations in which many do not survive. He instilled in me the resiliency to be a warrior and one who does not give up no matter what the circumstances. I am humbled by His grace and mercy.

To all the clients whom I provided services for 27 years when working in the field of social services, and in remembrance of those who passed away whom I had the honor of providing services for.

&

To my four children. Thank you for blessing me as your mother.

Table of Contents

Getting Started

A Story

How We Care About Ourselves Reflects Who We Are

Tools You Need

Maintenance/Managing

Quotes Cited/References/Resources Tools

Jeremiah 29:11

"For I know the plans I have for you," declares the Lord,
"plans to prosper you and not to harm you,
plans to give you hope and a future."

Preface

In life, we go through many different circumstances or phases, and some are more difficult than others. We learn through trials, errors, and mistakes that we make along life's journey. Life's mistakes can be productive if you embrace what they are teaching you. The important thing is to learn that what matters and what makes a difference in our lives is what we do during these trials and errors, determining either a positive or negative outcome. The process can easily discourage you and make you feel like you want to give up, especially during those hard-to-deal trials that challenge us and bring us into despair. When we have either failed or are on the brink of failing because of some bad decisions that we made. Our first reaction is to want to throw in the towel and give up. But what if we decide not to? What if we decide not to give up and instead get back up again, be restored, and continue pursuing our dreams? We often hear of so many successful stories of individuals who have achieved their dreams after failing many times, and just when they were about to throw it all away, a breakthrough happens. Sometimes we have big dreams, goals, or visions of things that we hope to do or accomplish. But we lack a road map on how to do it, the timing of when is the right moment to start working on our goals, or lack the knowledge of how to maintain sustainability once you accomplish it. Sometimes, we don't even know what tools we will need to make it happen. We only have a basic idea of what we want to achieve, or we have a dream but lack the guidance or vision, not knowing what resources and tools we need to make it a success. Does this resonate with you? I know I have been there, and this is why I have developed this workbook guide especially for you from what I learned. The purpose is to assist you in creating your own road map with goals, vision, and mission that will help you make your dreams come true as well as exploring other areas like your values, past self-sabotage behaviors, and other barriers that have prevented you in the past from completing your goals. This guide will provide you with some golden nuggets of skills that will assist you in learning what tools you will need, what resources are available for you, who you need to connect with, and how to stay on track by creating your own strategic plan. This strategic plan will be based on how things are aligned in your life and will teach you how to use it to catapult you into creating the life you dream of. Like me, if you are a believer in Christ Jesus our Lord Savior, you want to make sure that every decision fits within your moral values and Christian principles. Always placing God first in every decision that you make. You will achieve everything that you set yourself to do with God's approval. One of my favorite Bible verses is Jeremiah 29:11 "For I know the plans that I have for you." God already knows the plans that are best for our lives, and He desires for us to include Him in them.

This book is not only for believers in Christ but for anyone who needs a wholesome and positive guidebook that will help them get a clearer vision of what they want to accomplish and how to do it. This book will not only help you in achieving your dreams of becoming a life coach but also provide you with a workbook to put into practice all the valuable lessons provided. This will allow you to use critical thinking and help you evaluate where you are and any changes that you must make. I am confident that you will extract some wisdom that will empower you to live the life you want to live and be who you want to become. Many blessings! ~Claribel Coreano

> *"Getting started is the first step to knowing when to start working on your dreams is the key that will ignite the passion to continue taking other steps. And to know when to take action that will push towards the pathway of your dreams"* -Claribel Coreano

Introduction

My name is Claribel Coreano. I am a Transformational Life Coach, Writer, and Artist. My goal is to provide you with some tools and practice to help guide you along the road to accomplishing your dreams. First, I would like to share a little snippet of my bio. I am a native of the Dominican Republic, born in Santiago. I moved to New York City with my family at the age of eight years old. We then relocated to Connecticut after six years of living in Manhattan 17th and 19th off 9th Avenue in New York City. I lived in Connecticut until relocating to Florida on May 29th, 2021. I made this transition to move to Florida and have been here ever since. Prior to moving to Florida, I had been working on my dreams of becoming a life coach since 2011. I started slowly by taking training as I was still actively working in my position of Sr. Director of Clinical Services for Permanent Supportive Housing Programs. Yes, I never was one for titles, and I never felt comfortable with saying this one. Even during training or meetings, it was a mouth full. It's funny because when they created the title, it had to be one that encompassed all the roles and tasks I was responsible for, and this one just about covered them all. I want to clarify that I did this during my spare time as I was not yet clear on what path to take. I would also like to share a little about myself and what I have gone through in my own life.

My story is one of overcoming challenges, resilience, and determination. I married young as a teenager and became a high school dropout after becoming pregnant with my first child. After having my second child, and becoming a single mother, I obtained my GED and also applied for citizenship. No one provided me with information about what I had to do as an immigrant, even though when we first arrived in the US, we were granted a naturalization visa under my grandfather who was a United Citizen and a member of the military service in the US. I proudly completed my application, was interviewed after three months in Hartford, CT. I was quizzed on United States history, and I felt that I was granted approval on this day. It was interesting because the same year I was granted my citizenship they had also granted many war refugees, asylum seekers, and immigrants from different parts of the world citizenship. Since the city in which I lived had the highest number of immigrants granted citizenship; the mayor conducted a special ceremony about a month after, at the local high school auditorium. It was exciting because the auditorium was full of people, and I felt that this was such a big accomplishment for me. I remember when I was called and given my US citizenship certificate. I was so proud of myself for accomplishing this goal.

During this time, I started my journey in overcoming negative life patterns in my life by going back to school to study administrative/ secretarial training which landed me a job working in a hospital medical records as an admissions clerk. After divorcing my first husband, I got married again after 5 ½ years of being single. I had two more children from this marriage and after my youngest child was born I started working on obtaining an Associate degree as well as a one-year certification in Mental Health and Theory Practices. After completing my Associate's Degree, I took a break for several years to work supporting my family. After 14 years in a tumultuous domestic violence marriage, I knew that I had to go back to school to be able to improve my life and better able to financially support my children. It wasn't until after my divorce that I considered going back to school. I received my Bachelor's Degree in Human Services from Belhaven Christian College and then continued onto a Master's Degree in Human Services with concentration on Marriage & Family Therapy from the Cappella University in 2007. I am a life learner and love to learn new things, so I started my journey of learning more about life coaching in 2011. I completed several life coach certifications, including a one-year certification from the Southwest Institute of Healing Arts, Tempe, Arizona in 2015. Additional certifications include becoming a Certified Life Coaching NLP Certificate in 2011 and Women's Empowerment Life Coaching in 2019. This set the ball rolling for me, and after leaving my position in May 2021, I made the decision that I wanted to help others in a different way. I worked in the social services field for over 27 years, working first with the HIV/Aids population. When I first began my career, it was during the beginning of the epidemic, and after three years, I changed to working with the homeless population, those suffering from mental health issues, substance abuse, and other socioeconomic problems. I have worked with individuals, youth, veterans, families, and criminal justice clients in many different roles. The skill set of effective listening and asking open-ended questions I had used in many of the interventions with my past clients. Remarkably, similar to life coaching guidance except it was behavioral and clinical interventions.

On a personal level, I raised four sons, one of whom has served the country in active war conflict in Afghanistan for three years and is now an Army disabled veteran. My oldest is a coordinator for a health care agency, my third son is a licensed optical design and dispensing optical center manager, and my youngest is a successful business owner and personal trainer. In my spare time, I dedicate myself to my hobbies which are writing and painting. I remember that as a child I was always drawing in my notebooks. My interest in painting was already there but not fully developed. I started painting in 2002 and progressively got better skilled in painting. I consider myself an intuitive artist, and this is because I have not been professionally trained as a painter. Most of my paintings come from my imagination and with no training or knowledge of mixing colors and painting techniques. I have developed my own style by using different mediums of texture, paper, napkins, aluminum, gesso, and glue. For painting I use knives, my fingers, quit tips, pencils, needles, and of course, brushes to achieve what I visualize in my mind. The final colors come gradually as I add them until they become the right color then, I know that it is completed. I am also more of an eclectic painter because I just don't paint one style but focus on whatever I visualize in my imagination and then transfer it onto the canvas. Why do I paint? It helps me relax and visualize something beautiful then transfer into a canvas. Writing has always been a passion of mine since young. I have been writing poetry and journaling and wrote a poetry book in 2006 - which I am working on revising and republishing again.

Why did I want to become a coach? I wanted to help others who had experienced trauma and domestic violence and who are single mothers who are raising children on their own. As a domestic violence survivor and childhood trauma survivor, I have never considered myself a victim but always a survivor. I know firsthand what is needed to overcome obstacles, negative mindsets, trauma, and abuse. I learned how to defeat these setbacks, all of which I was able to overcome with the help of counselors and life coaching. Resiliency has allowed me to overcome many hardships I faced in my life. And it has become my mission to help others build resiliency, become empowered, and gain self-esteem to help them live their best lives. My life has been a testament to the strength of the human spirit and the power of God's love, and I hope to inspire others who are facing similar difficulties. I experienced many difficulties throughout my life, but I am happy to say that throughout all these trials God provided me with the courage and hope that I needed. Life has not been easy for me; however, I gained a lot of wisdom from all of my experiences. I consider myself a truly fortunate individual. I am a survivor! As a result of all these experiences. I felt inspired to share what I have accomplished as a young mother, experiencing domestic violence, raising my children, learning about relationships, and accepting everything as a lesson learned.

The wisdom gained from surviving childhood trauma, PTSD, domestic violence, experiencing health issues, raising children as a single parent, and overcoming financial hardship has afforded me with a chest full of wisdom, resiliency, and empathy. These are the tools that life has afforded me and that are valuable impartations of hope and strengths that I intend to share with others to assist them in becoming empowered, learning how to thrive, and overcoming every situation that has been a barrier or obstacle in their lives. These are my paying it forward, my gifts and my blessings to share to help empower others.

My Experience and Expertise

"Sometimes we don't really see how valuable life lessons are until we use them to help others. By imparting the wisdom and experience gained, we teach others how to grow from the pain of the lessons learned. We are not taught to heal but to thrive.
What if I told you we can do both and work daily on our healing? Knowing that there is hope in healing, they will learn how to prevent it the second time around." —Claribel Coreano

Sometimes we don't realize the value of life lessons until we learn the purpose of why things had to happen the way they did. It has allowed me to gain many skills in overcoming adversities. Through these hard lessons, I became more skilled in resiliency, working on becoming more self-confident, how to distinguish my triggers, and most importantly, I learned how to have self-compassion, thrive, and heal from trauma. All of which I was able to achieve through my faith and belief in a higher power. I learned how to trust in God, trust the guidance of therapists, and was helped by several life coaches. These coaches came from different niches and backgrounds but uniquely taught me many different tips on becoming healed and ways to manage the trauma as well as how to continue on my healing journey beyond. As a result of all the positive people who have entered my life and helped me, it has become my mission to help others learn how to build resiliency, become empowered, and gain self-esteem to permit them to live their best lives. Today, I am most grateful for each and every one of these amazing individuals who touched my life in one way or another.

Although I have spent half of my lifetime recovering from childhood trauma, domestic violence, and other difficulties, I am here to tell you today that trauma did not stop me! I also testify that during my healing journey it never stopped me from becoming an empowered woman, nor has it deterred me from accomplishing all my dreams of becoming a life coach. Looking back on everything that God has allowed me to accomplish and what I have survived in my life, not only have these achievements demonstrated the resiliency inside me to not allow the trauma to define me but also the ability for it to be the catalyst of growth. One way that this unfolded was working in a helping profession for so many years. I feel that it was another way that God allowed me to not only help others but also heal while doing it.

I am grateful to God for allowing me to experience that phase of my life because I was able to witness firsthand those suffering trauma at many different levels and struggling with other dysfunctions that affected their daily lives. It always made me reflect on the fact that their struggles, pasts, and traumas were way more complex than mine, making me feel ever so grateful for what God had already done in my life. Despite all the different stories I witnessed and the extremely dangerous circumstances I was exposed to when servicing these vulnerable individuals, I still believed that I was there to share hope and encouragement with them so that they too could heal. Again, the lessons learned made me stronger and more determined to make a difference in people's lives and continue to heal myself. I gained a lot of wisdom and skills from all the experiences life afforded me. I consider myself an extremely fortunate individual in the sense that not only was I a vessel in teaching others to heal but a healed survivor who is now completely thriving as a healed person. This is why I felt inspired to share some of the skills I gained with others who may be experiencing or have experienced trauma, domestic violence, or any other hardships. Through my life coaching services, I intend to teach individuals new ways that will not only incite healing and personal growth but will also allow them to learn how to thrive and lead a more productive life.

How did I start in the helping profession? Well, I remember when I was in college, I became involved in the student development office, providing support to other students as well as helping other students on subjects with which they were struggling. Another training camp for me in my life coaching journey has been working in the social work field. The vast human interaction with clients, staff, and providers during my professional experience afforded me the gift of learning about human behavior. Working with direct services, groups, and psychiatric interventions allowed me the opportunity to learn more about human behavior, family dysfunctions, relationship dynamics, and many other areas such as substance abuse, addictive personalities, the mentally disabled, and individuals who were lacking daily living skills or financial management. Many of the clients experienced major traumatic events, CPTSD, dysfunction, generational cycles of abuse, trauma, and cyclical history of homelessness as well as learned helplessness. These resulted in them needing psychiatric interventions, clinical social worker guidance, medical intervention, and vocational rehabilitation in order to enhance their quality of life. Again, valuable learning opportunities for any life coach to have; in fact, many LCSW or Ph.D. social workers are shifting careers to life coaching because it allows them to guide clients in a more proactive manner that empowers them to heal and lead a more productive life.

This exposure allowed me the creativity and flexibility during this phase of my life to not only create different programming to meet clients' needs but also effective interventions, policies, and procedures that would help increase the clients' quality of life. It has also allowed me to gain a wealth of experience and be able to manage a business effectively. Having been exposed to several different roles, responsibilities, and levels of management has afforded me the knowledge and practice to coach others. For example, in my leadership role as clinical director and supervisor, I was able to learn many different aspects of being an emotionally intelligent leader through continuous training and practice. I was able to manage the supervision of staff, create clinical orientation manuals, and oversee new employee training. I was also coaching and training staff on how to conduct a clinical intervention, conduct psychosocial assessments, write documentation, and do stakeholder reporting. I worked collaboratively with hospitals, mental health rehabilitation, behavioral centers, psychiatrists, psychologists, clinical social workers, and pharmacists, facilitating treatment and crisis intervention meetings. The second exposure came about from the financial business aspect of non-profit supervisory management which consists of managing financial budgets for several housing programs including writing several government grant funding for a criminal justice vocational program, grant reporting, and entering financial budgets during fiscal year dues and programming data in funder websites. This allowed me to gain knowledge in many different business theory practices, data entry, reporting, purchasing, ordering accounts receivable, and reconciliation.

This intense training included learning how a business operates by attending supervisory and leadership management training, joining the leadership cohort at the local university, and passing and becoming certified by the national headquarters office in leadership. As a result of this, I was also assigned to work with human resources as a participant in a subcommittee to assist in creating policies and procedures and conduct employee satisfaction surveys. I also became part of the employee star committee that evaluated employee satisfaction and worked on creating positive morale in the company to ensure that all employees were valued and celebrated. This allowed me the opportunity to be part of the revamping of HR hiring practices, employee applications, orientation process video making, and other activities. As part of my position, I conducted behavioral interviews and processed new hire documentation. This experience allowed me to recognize staff contributions and celebrate those who worked for the company for several years. This skill will help me in my own business once it grows by hiring staff. This versatility also allowed me to learn property management skills during the latter part of my employment history there. I took on this role for eight years as a property manager for three subsidized properties in addition to my position of sr. clinical director for PSH programs. This position allowed the opportunity to work closely with the Section 8 office, a federally funded program that assists clients with rental payments. In the role of property manager, I had to learn about all the facets of federal housing programs, Section 8 documentation, stakeholders, rent reconciliation, monthly reporting, and develop a good network of lawyers to support and build relationships with other landlords from the community. As part of this role, I was responsible for creating lease agreements/signing, tenant screenings, orientations, occupancy certificates, Section 8 inspection, and the last process of completing all the Section 8 documentation for all new move-ins and then sending it to their office for subsidy processing and approvals. This required not only screening one applicant but sometimes several at the same time to ensure subsidy payments were received in a timely manner at the main office.

In addition to all these tasks, I also supervised maintenance staff and oversaw that all property repairs were conducted promptly. This process required accepting bids from contractors, purchasing major equipment, and paying vendors for unit preparation for new move-ins. For one of the programs, I had the honor of coordinating the grand opening and ribbon cutting of a newly developed family housing program. This is just an example of the many different skills that I learned as a program director and sr. clinical director. The field of social work, especially working with the homeless or housing, requires that you wear many different hats and take on many different responsibilities to ensure the success of the programs. The human services field is not a glamorous job; you actually have to be open to being in the trenches, getting your hands dirty, and really being involved in all aspects of the clients' lives as a permanent housing provider feeding the homeless, distributing donations, and other client related events. As a supervisor, I worked hard to create a healthy and positive work culture and be a role model for my staff. I started as a case manager, then sr. case manager, lead case manager, program director, to my last position as Sr. Clinical Director for Permanent Supportive Housing Programs. This shows that I worked really hard to get to my last position and being a leader throughout the majority of my work history. You may think that all these skills are not related to life coaching, but in reality, it demonstrates the many tools that I can creatively use to help others who may need the support in any of these areas.

Why do I mention all of these different roles and responsibilities? Because this wisdom alone has helped me with learning about myself and others and how I can help guide people as a life coach. I learned that the best way to engage the clients is to meet them where they are, build rapport with them, and gain their trust in order for them to open up about their situations. Being present and genuine is especially important when dealing with any client population by demonstrating respect and seeing them as human beings, not just a diagnosis or their struggles. I hold these valuable lessons dear to my heart because I have learned to see and love others through the eyes of Christ. These experiences allowed me to learn more about how to be an effective and reflective listener as well as gain knowledge regarding the many resources that helped empower my clients and the appropriate support that will help enhance their quality of living. I value and honor the wealth of wisdom gained, and I am extremely grateful for all the different opportunities I have had working with many different populations throughout my career. After 28 years, I decided to make a shift in my career by helping people at a different level and becoming an entrepreneur by starting my own business. It has been a different journey of learning with new territory, skills, and environments.

Why Coaching?

"Coaching is not a one-size-fits-all, or better yet said, not a fix-all. No, the clients have to do the work by taking action steps, accepting accountability, and becoming committed to working on themselves. They must reach self-discoveries into their own healing and personal growth. It has amazing results if it is dually proactive!"
—Claribel Coreano

Why did I decide on coaching? Well, coaching has always been something I wanted to do and have been informally doing - not only with friends and family but also with past clients in the role of a diabetes prevention wellness coach and as a vocational and educational coach. In a prior position, I coached, supervised, and mentored many university student interns from an associate-level to master-level programs every semester. And throughout the years of working in the field, I was also able to supervise and coach maturity elderly workers for a 55 and over "reintegration to the workforce" program. In my role as a leader, I completed several training on employee coaching, emotional intelligence, and behavioral interviewing to effectively supervise staff and develop leaders. My style of supervision involved coaching staff during supervision, yearly evaluations, as well as creating a development plan for growth that included educational and training goals every year. My main focus was to help staff grow in their careers in the agency and for them to complete their educational goals so that they could move up the ladder in the company. I have also informally coached and mentored several of my friends during their process of starting their own businesses or when making career changes. I decided that it was now time to take it to the next level - start my own business and put all my gifts and talents to use in the field of life coaching.

Why is coaching not a one-size-fits-all, or better yet, not a fix-all? People desire choices in the type of services that they are looking for. This means that a person who suffered from trauma will not do well with a coach who specializes only in business because their approach may not be what the person needs. People want someone who they can connect with or who can relate to their sufferings, problems, struggles, careers, or needs that they are seeking assistance for. Similarly, the clients have to be intentional in wanting to do the work and taking actionable steps toward learning new ways to manage or heal from their trauma. For example, they have to be open to accepting accountability that this is indeed what they desire and are ready to heal. They must decide to confront it and acknowledge that it did happen, but they will no longer let it control them or run their life and stop them from healing. This is when they will obtain a healing breakthrough and will be set on their way to being free from the bondage that trauma causes in a person. I learned that a person can only overcome trauma when he or she desires to heal and is committed to working on themselves. This is important because the healing journey is not an easy one; therefore, they must be really serious and committed to their healing. It is all about being guided toward learning some ways to heal, gaining insight on their self-discoveries, and continuing to take action towards healing and personal growth.

When I started authoring this book, I did not know which way it was going to go. So, I started reflecting on my own life experiences, my journey in becoming a life coach, and I decided that I wanted to help others who may encounter the very same things that I struggled with during this phase of my career change. I also want to share the wealth of knowledge and experience gained throughout my life. I had to make several adjustments in life and also take a leap of faith to start working on this new chapter of my life, which is to become a life coach as well as the embodiment of encouragement for all whom I will serve. Another reason is that, all my life, I have always helped people. Becoming a life coach will allow me to continue to help others in a different manner, teaching them to grow and become a better version of themselves. Taking this big step in my life has been brought about in part by the changes that I myself underwent not only in my personal life but also in my career, financially as well as in a change of physical location. Starting my own business brought about many changes, obstacles, and barriers that helped me in learning more skills through trial and error. I learned to not only maneuver on my own but also to stay humble. When I got to a point of needing support, I searched to find the appropriate assistance.

- I first started by seeking life coaching services to discuss my goals with a life coach and obtain guidance from the coach as to how to start once I was ready to take the leap into the world of life coaching. My coach provided me with motivation and encouragement to get things started once I moved to Florida, as I was already working on my move to Florida. His coaching set the first step towards bringing my dreams to life and offered me constructive feedback that allowed me to find my own answers. He also guided me with the move transition to evaluate the positive and negative, again this helped me with making the final decision.

- The second step was for me to write my goals down on paper with a timeline of target dates and tasks. I started with writing down my vision and mission with a description of each and how it reflects the services that I will be providing.

- The third step was creating a business plan that allowed me to keep tabs on tasks, deadlines, action steps, and revisions if things took longer than expected. The business plan helped me stay accountable for each task and accomplish things in order of priority.

- The fourth thing he suggested was to speak with other coaches and get feedback from them. I was able to speak with several coaches to obtain their take on life coaching and how they are managing their businesses.

- The fifth was looking for assistance with the branding, business cards, and marketing. This turned out better than I expected because it was also a learning curve for me and a lesson learned. I had an idea of what I was looking for when I met with a marketing business coach, and she was able to create my branding colors, logos, and business cards professionally. I was pleased with the final product because it represents my branding.

All of these resources and support help me in keeping me aligned with both my personal and business goals. Seeking support makes the transitioning process much easier. And you also learn valuable information from other coaches.

The journey has not been all that easy. Through sweat and tears I pushed through. Through self-doubts, feeling unprepared, experiencing medical hardship, and almost feeling like quitting at times. I kept pushing forward, and even when it felt like I was getting nowhere, with God's guidance and direction, I learned not only to trust and depend solely on Him but also to learn from others through networking and asking questions. I was able to quickly find the answers I was seeking, find the resources and support, or be kindly guided in the right direction by other coaches. I want to encourage everyone who is looking to start this journey that you too can do it, but you have to stay focused on your goals and not give up. No matter how difficult the journey becomes and what you face, continue to pray for it and push through until you see the end results. Stay disciplined, consistent, and determined. This is why I authored this book as a golden nugget of motivation and encouragement for others to stay encouraged and focused in their journey.

How Did I Start My Journey?

"Starting a new journey in life can be difficult and challenging, but in the end, you look back and think, 'That is who I was, that was where I have been, this is where I am now, and this who I am becoming!' It was all worth it!" —Claribel Coreano

How did I start my journey? Well, I started by moving to another state and starting a new life. I followed God's prompting to leave everything behind and start with a blank slate. I started with getting rid of the bulky stuff in my apartment by donating and selling some items. I remember the day that I placed all of the remaining furniture, dishes, pots and pans, bed frames, and living room items outside in the city where I lived back in Connecticut for anyone to take for free. Why did I do this? I felt God prompting me to do so, to leave everything behind, and so I did. It just so happened that everyone who took items told me how much they needed them and that it was a blessing. One particular individual cried as she shared her story of how she was homeless and had just secured an apartment near the city in which I lived, and she basically needed all the household items that I was giving away. She told me it was a blessing from God and that God was going to bless me for this. I know that I may sound crazy to some people, but I knew that this was God's confirmation and obedience when He told me to leave everything behind. We never know how God is going to be glorified unless we are obedient to what He is calling us to do. I am glad I did. As I was blessing others, I knew that God would bless me in my new location.

I moved to my new location on May 29, 2021, and God blessed me with everything I needed and more. I found a beautiful house to rent with furniture which I bought from the owner at a reasonable price including pots, dishes, utensils, and appliances. It was a gift from God as God provided everything I gave away with better and higher-end quality.

11 months after moving to my new location, I lost my father on April 29, 2022 due to cancer. The grieving process itself was not easy and it took a toll on me that whole year. Then, in October 2022, I fell and suffered a head injury again - another setback, although it was minor. It still caused me headaches, foggy brain, and difficulties with my speech for a few months. This added to so many other trials, testing, and situations that I had encountered during that year. Normally, these would have made anyone quit or give up. I battled health issues as a result of the aftermath of the Covid-19 vaccination which precipitated an autoimmune disorder, bouts of losing my hair, and several other health problems on top of grieving, all while I was still working on my dream. I will tell you that God in His mercy and grace have given me the strength to roll with the punches and make lemonade with the lemons that life has handed me. I realized that while I may have experienced all that and then some, I felt that I was out of my job season. I decree and declare it in Jesus's name: "No victim here, just a victorious woman of God." You see, God wants me to continue to speak life. And why not? Because all the lessons in my journey have a divine purpose for testimonies so others can heal. How else will people see and acknowledge that it was God, has been God all along working in my life, and is still God's doing now? Know this: I had the choice to become bitter, angry, or retaliate, but God said no! Instead, I will turn it out for your good. Here's why. He has blessed me with many encouraging words, testimonies, and experiences that He wants me to share.

These experiences, testimonies, and encouraging words are not because of me, but because of Him working in my life, and for His name to be glorified through it all. Every word that He has given me has been Holy Spirit-inspired. How can I best explain it? Well, because everything we experience in life is to build our faith, and this is where others who lack faith will see God's goodness. You may ask, how come you have such a strong faith in God? I can only speak about the fact that the process of pain, loss, rejection, abuse, and so many other circumstances that I have been through have made me realize that He never left me or forsaken me. Romans 15:13 states, "May the God of hope fill you with all the joy and peace as you trust in him, so that you may overflow with hope by the power of the Holy Spirit." My life has been a true testament to the power of God's love in my life and of how He has kept me. Like the story of Job, many were quick to point fingers or even question his plight. And that is ok. I often question it myself because I am amazed by God's miracles in my life. You may say, Hogwash, she couldn't possibly have been able to survive all that. Again, I also question that myself but also with immense gratitude to God. This is where the faith part comes in. God built that faith in me through all these trials and testing. I went through the furnace and came out unscathed. My faith in Him has been as strong as it is now. And the pain I had endured will only bring Him glory. John 16:33 NIV "In this world you will have trouble. But take heart! I have overcome the world." This is to give God the glory and praise. I glorify His holy name.

When I started the journey of starting my business and authoring this book, I did not understand the purpose behind this then, but I do now. You see, God did not want anyone else to take credit for what he was about to do with my life. He was going to be glorified in my life no matter the circumstances or difficulties that I had encountered. He was going to make sure that people notice the differences from where I started to where I am now. This is the only way people would have recognized that His hands were directing my path and that only He had the blueprints and plans for my life. He knew which way I needed to go. So here I am, starting from a blank slate to blessings! With God, anything is possible when we allow Him to direct our steps. And so far, God has been there for me, guiding and protecting me in the right direction. Let me remind you to celebrate the small victories as if they were huge victories because it is by expressing gratitude for the small things that

God moves and works in our life to bring forth the bigger blessings. Now, let's get into the theoretical definition, component and role of coaching, and practice and of establishing a life coaching business.

What is the Difference Between a Coach or Therapist?

"A therapist is someone who conducts in-depth psychoanalysis of your life and helps you learn and manage a mental illness, personality disorder, or family dysfunction. On the other hand, a coach is like a compass who can help you find barriers, weaknesses, and deficiencies through your own guided self-discovery. The coach then guides you on how you can work on them or implement new skills so that it can catapult you into growth or in making adequate changes."
—Claribel Coreano

What is coaching and what is it not? Let me explain. A good coach is like a teacher; you are teaching your clients but allowing them the autonomy to find what it is that they need to change in themselves or their careers, lives, relationships, families, and businesses. The client then learns how to apply what they learn about themselves and make the necessary changes. A coach allows their clients to see the bigger picture in order for them to make future decisions. One way that the coach achieves this is by building trust and rapport with the client. One of the most important functions of a coach is to first build the engagement conversation by asking them where they have been. It offers an opportunity for the coach to have awareness on what insights the client gained from their past experiences, if any, if they were valuable for them, and what skills they learn from them. As a coach, your main function is to encourage your clients to make shifts towards their own self-discovery by asking them empowering and probing questions that promote self-autonomy, helping them find their own answers. Thus, you are offering encouragement that helps them look inward for their own answers without offering them the solutions, instead challenging them enough so that they can find the solutions within. It is a process of empowering the individual to become more self-aware, confident, and able to recognize triggers that project past defeats, mistakes, or behaviors. It is about encouraging reflective internal dialogue that will help them bring awareness to their presenting issues that they need to address and work on with the coach. The coach offers insights that will help them take actions to move forward and evaluate if they are committed to doing the work it takes to change as well as asking what other supports that they will need to be successful.

A coach uses many different tools to facilitate clarification. For example, tools, models, instruments, assessments, theories, quizzes, questions, and surveys. These tools are instrumental in inciting critical thinking which allows them to gain deep insight about themselves, others, and the decisions they must make. These tools are just as important as the tools that a surgeon uses to operate. If these tools are not organized and in order, they are not able to operate. Without them, they cannot operate as they are designed. Just as it is necessary to conduct an incision in a specific area of the body in order to help the person heal, the surgeon must remove the disease that is affecting the person. This works in the same way a coach uses their tools to help the clients remove whatever is causing barriers, stress, or stagnation. Sometimes the coach will not know what specific tools to use until the client discloses a specific issue or problem. For example, for a client who refers to feeling overwhelmed and not knowing how to find life balance. The wheel of life exercise tool is instrumental in helping the client measure different areas of their lives in different categories in which they feel that they are struggling with. The client will then evaluate where he or she is in each area of their life and grade it by a number. By shading the areas with the number assigned, the client will have a clearer picture of where they are in each area. After finishing the exercise the client will reach self-discovery by finding out that what they felt was their presenting problem is probably not the priority but something else is. At this point the client will share on each area and why they grade with a certain number and what must they do to increase the number in order to have life balance. This process will go on until all areas of life are discussed and what the clients share on taking action to raise the number. The lowest area the client soon will discover is the number one priority that they need to work on to reach a healthy balanced life.

The coach, just like a therapist, follows a set of guidelines, ethical procedures, as well as confidentiality guidelines. While many coaches become certified by the International Coaching Federation, or the International Christian Coaching Institute they are not licensed like a therapist. A coach may have his or her own practice but not accept private insurance as it is not a clinical setting. Now, let's learn about the difference between the two. A therapist has to have a license to practice and be under the supervision of a doctoral level supervisor depending on their degree. The therapist offers clinical intervention in a clinical setting, licensed by the city or state in which they practice, and sometimes may have more than one license to practice in two or more states. Many accept different types of insurance as they are a licensed clinical practice and also have additional insurance coverage for the whole practice itself. The model of intervention use is based on the school of thought that the clinical social worker or therapist specializes in, and their specialty is based on the therapist's interest to provide services to the specific population along with extensive experience and specialization. For example, they may specialize in DBT (Dialectical Behavioral Therapy) or Cognitive Behavioral Therapy, amongst many others. Both are good therapeutic models of intervention for clients who have suffered major trauma, PTSD, lack of impulse, or other cognitive limitations. It is important to know that when you become a coach you have to make an assessment decision and evaluate if a client is a good fit for life coaching. If the person is presenting or needs clinical intervention, you can then refer them to a clinical specialist for the proper treatment.

A coach can reject clients needing psychological treatment as opposed to coaching for several reasons. One reason is conflict of interest, as it is not a clinical setting, and their presenting problem is more clinical than life coaching can provide. Secondly, licensure may be a factor. Life coaching does not require a license. Third, safety risks could be involved as the individual may be a threat to themselves or others, placing themselves and the coach in harm's way. And fourth, HIPAA restrictions due to the nature of the situation along with not accepting insurance could be reasons to decline. The life coach is required to be transparent with the individual and inform them of the policies and procedures for their business. However, clients can receive coaching if they are referred by their own therapist, clinical social worker, or psychiatrist, along with their required therapy, to work on a specific life skills problem as long as they are considered stable in both their medication and mental health treatment and deemed as ready for life skills coaching. Possible combined releases of information may be signed for both coaching and clinical support as they will need to discuss life skills or occupational rehabilitation goals that they will be working on. Otherwise, it is not recommended for any persons who are still not mentally or medically stable in treatment nor cognitively able to stay committed to making changes in themselves. Another restriction is, who will be paying for the services? Will the client be responsible or will a third-party be the payee? I know from experience in the social services field that there may be some programs that pay for holistic services which life coaching may fall under life skills, life coaching, stress management, or relaxation and for those who practice hypnotherapy. If there are still any such existing programs available now, they will have to be an approved business based on the grant or funding the payor agency description falls under services provided. This is not set in stone. I am sharing this as an example based on programs that I used in the past for my clients. For example, for the AIDS population, there were such paid services in the past as well as for clients coming out of the criminal justice system. There were approved vocational and life skills agencies that paid for these types of services as long as they met the agency guidelines and requirement for contract services for life skills or holistic services. Again, this is just an example of a third-party payor. Otherwise, the person is solely responsible to pay for the services.

Now, let's explore what makes a client ready for coaching. What makes them a good fit for coaching? In the following pages, I developed some questions to help you evaluate if you or someone is ready to receive coaching.

Are You Ready to Receive Coaching?

"In life you may never be fully ready, but you must take a leap of faith and say you are ready and believe you are ready. Then be committed that you said you are ready, because now your words become contractual, and you must follow through with being ready. It's like you think about it, ok, you made the first call and ask questions; this is when you are contemplating and now you must say yes or no. If yes, then you showed interest. The next step is taking action by showing the commitment to lock into the session and keep up with their appointments. The most important part of being ready is that of being committed. Commitment to attend all of your sessions and to stay fully committed comes when it is time to make those hard to do changes that come with the growing pains. On another note, this is where the life coach showcases her services to the client and demonstrates how he or she will coach the client in the areas they feel they need coaching on." —Claribel Coreano

How can you know if you are ready? How can you know if you yourself can benefit from coaching? First and foremost, you must evaluate your personal level of needs and your interest in making changes in your own life. You must continuously work on yourself to better understand your clients and improve your quality of providing the best services to them. Yes, you must evaluate if your challenges are coachable or if they require additional support from a life coach. How can you know the difference? If you are currently inexperienced in some areas as a coach, let's perhaps say organization or dealing with the business aspect of the coaching business, it is best to obtain support from a coach who is experienced in those areas so that they can guide you in improving those areas. Coaches need coaches to guide them in their business so that they can have a sounding board to fall on when they need support. It is advisable for coaches to see other coaches as a practical way of staying grounded and maintaining clarity on what they do, offer, and are passionate about. Yes, there will be times during which you may encounter a challenging client and need sound advice from others who have been there and done that so that they can share how they handled it, what worked for them, and if it is an ethical or moral issue. This is just to help the coach protect their practice, provide sound advice, and follow the International Life Coach Ethical Guidelines according to the International Coaching Federation. Now, let's discuss what will make a client ready or not ready for life coaching.

A ready client will be a client who matches the services that you are providing and who is able to be committed to doing the work necessary to change those areas of their lives based on what they themselves have discovered needing the assistance on. The client will be able to choose a coach and be committed to paying for their coaching. On the other hand, a client who presents with debilitating depression or any other mental illness that interferes with their daily life or with their decision making will not be a good fit for coaching. It is important that you refer them to follow-up with mental health support as opposed to coaching them. To better understand if the person calling you for services needs more than what you can offer them as their coach, or if they need clinical support and are just not ready for life coaching, here are some questions that will be able to help see if they are a good fit or not for life coaching. These questions can be part of your intake process as well.

1. Are you experiencing any unusual behaviors that you feel are out of your control right now? Do these behaviors interfere with your daily life? If so, do they affect your thought process or your ability to make decisions? Are the behaviors making you exhibit any unusual behaviors that you are not sure about? Do you experience other symptoms?

If the client shows evidence of needing clinical support, then you can discuss with them your concerns and let them know that they are not appropriate for your services. You can either direct them to someone who does offer those services or provide them with a hotline number they can call where they can obtain the proper services that they need at that particular moment. No matter how detailed your website may be on what you offer, there are still individuals who may want to call a life coach even when their struggles are more difficult than the services you offer because of the stigma that has been placed on seeking mental health support.

The coach will need to evaluate if the person calling for services is able to manage his or her symptoms without needing the additional support of medication or clinical therapy. Let's say they are someone who has been psychologically stable for years and no longer receiving medication treatment. For example, some individuals who suffer from ADHD or neurodivergent disorders may struggle with their thought process and in making decisions but qualify for life coaching.

Then, you can let them know that you may not be the appropriate coach for them and refer them to someone who can meet their needs.

2. Are you feeling stuck in past trauma or unresolved issues that require a more in-depth analysis of your life?

Let's say a person calls you and wants you as a life coach. They tell you that they want to work on a specific area - let's say trauma. And as a coach, you do not work with clients in this area. Since it is not your specialty, and you normally work with clients who are looking into making career changes and other personal life changes, you may need to reject the client.

In another scenario, the person describes the plethora of unresolved traumatic events which he or she discloses never obtaining any clinical counseling on and begins describing that it is affecting all areas of their lives, describing depression, substance use, and/or other psychological symptoms requiring more in-depth analysis. Definitely not a client that is ready for coaching; again, follow the same protocol of referring them to the appropriate services.

3. Have you recently been under the care of a psychiatrist or psychologist? If so, where, when, and why?

Again, this question should be part of your intake process, and this will help you determine if the client is ready or not.

4. Are you currently being or have been prescribed psychotropic medications or are under the care of a psychologist or psychiatrist?

Again, this question should be part of your intake process, and this will help you determine if the client is ready or not.

5. Are you fully committed to working with a life coach? If so, can you describe how ready you feel, and why? What are you willing to do for yourself to make these changes?

This question will determine the client's ability to be motivated for change. The process of change involves differentiation between wanting change, being ready for change, being committed to change, being proactive, and taking action to change.

6. Are you able to make decisions in your life that will require you to make changes in behaviors, ways of thinking, and managing triggers or habits?

Again, these types of questions determine the client's ability to be motivated for change. The process of change involves differentiation between wanting change, being ready for change, being committed to change, being proactive, and taking action to change.

7. Are you open and committed to working with a life coach in making these changes? If so, can you describe why and how it will help you?

Again, if the client is not open or committed to changing to working with a life coach in making these changes they will not produce growth. I found an amazing tool titled "How Coachable Are You?" It provides that client with a score on their readiness to be a coach and allows the opportunity to discuss the scores with the coach to work on the areas that they show deficiency and why. It can be a coaching session that will help the client change some negative fears of change.

8. What are the three most important areas that you desire to work with a coach in order of priority? And why?

Now, this one is planting the seed to learn how to set goals and also providing the client with the autonomy to find what takes priority in their life at this particular moment. The client may report these areas as a priority but then make a self-discovery during the session that the area they prioritized is not the one they need to work on. Again, this is where the coach can explore with the client during the free coaching session by conducting an exercise tool that helps them explore this more in depth.

There is one specific tool that I like using, which is the wheel of life, because it measures all areas from life, relationship, health, career, education finances, family, and spirituality. It's a great one to use as the client makes their own discovery on areas which they felt insignificant to make changes may turn out to be the one that needs the most attention. It is one of the great many tools available to help the client explore more in depth where they want to work on with the life coach. Keep in mind that some clients may have great insight on themselves and know specifically what area they want to work on at that specific moment.

These are all important and helpful questions to ask to see if you are a good fit for the client or if they are ready for life coaching. I will elaborate more in the next section, about being ready to be a coach or ready to become a life coach.

Are You Ready to Be a Coach?

"What makes you ready to be a coach is the desire and passion to help others learn about themselves and help them grow into their best version of themselves. Although you may never feel fully ready, you must take the plunge because this is something you have envisioned and created a mission for. It is now your time to rise up and do what you have been chosen and called to do."
—Claribel Coreano

Could you make a change in your life? If so, what will be the first step you wish to take? Could you see yourself ready to make the change? What are the steps that you would need to take? Are you ready to work on changing yourself for the better? Life coaching is an opportunity to work on areas that you yourself feel stuck in, don't know what to do with, or how to take the first step toward. Knowing how and what worked for you when you were stuck in this place is a tool for you to be able to help others in their own journey of change and of growth.

If the person is functioning stably without requiring a psychiatrist or psychologist, then they are ready for life coaching. If they are looking for insights on how to make changes in their career, relationship, and other aspects of their lives, then life coaching is a good fit for them. The changes that they seek to change or perhaps they have not yet discovered, but they will discover it during their life coaching session. An interesting fact about coaching is that sometimes a person may come in with a presenting problem or issues that they want clarification on, and it turns out to be a whole different issue that is causing the barriers or obstacles. Through different types of exploration exercises, clients may be able to pinpoint the primary issue in their life, and sometimes this will be the first area to work on with the life coach. Now that we are aware of what makes them ready or not for life coaching, we will begin discussing some tools for those who would like to be a life coach. What makes you a good life coach? Are you ready to be a life coach? What skills do you need to be a life coach? What makes a good life coach?

What makes a good life coach is their ability to listen effectively and be able to guide others in finding their own answers. A good life coach is always ready to coach others. You could be in a grocery store or any other locations and strike up a conversation that leads to an impromptu, mini coaching session that will result in more life coaching sessions. Life experience is a good toolbox of knowledge that will assist you in your life coaching journey. It could be as easy having extensive work knowledge of human resources, leadership, or hiring and training others. The skills that this type of work affords you can help in the areas of team building, personalities, work love languages, engaging employees, toxic work cultures, improving morale, and supervisory life skills coaching. There are many other areas that you can become an expert on. Know that no matter how good the life coach is, it is advisable to obtain life coaching experience to help you evaluate more in detail if this is indeed a good fit for you or if there are areas in your life that will need to work on. Also, it helps you refine some areas that may need improvement as well as obtaining coaching on how to start your own life coaching business. I myself obtained coaching from several coaches before plunging into the journey, and it helped me evaluate more about myself, what they do, and I was able to obtain proper guidance on what to do. It was all worth it.

In terms of schools that offer a life coaching program, I will share a little bit of my experience as I go along into more details in other chapters. Choosing a school is just as important; you will need to research to make sure that it is an accredited ICF life coaching school. There are many programs out there and you need to do your own research to know which one is a good fit for you as well as cost-effective for your budget.

There are many programs available that are costly or are part of the trainer's niche which may be relatable to yours. I myself chose a one-year program which afforded me a lot of great knowledge, practice, guidance, and expertise. Let's start this journey of a new beginning. In the following paragraphs, you will have the opportunity to not only learn some new practical skills in life coaching but to also put them into practice by using the skills you have learned from each chapter and then applying the lessons from each chapter using critical thinking by answering the questions at the end of each chapter. What does a new beginning look like to you? In the next chapter, we will learn more about new beginnings and why sometimes it is necessary as part of the process of making changes in preparation for your role as a life coach.

New Beginnings

"Why is a new beginning healthy? What does a new beginning look like for you? A new beginning doesn't necessarily mean moving to another physical location unless this is something that you have been pondering and planning on for a while. It could be as simple as moving to another city in your state or a new apartment or perhaps leaving a relationship, job, or changing career. How prepared do you feel to take the plunge into a new life?" —C.Coreano

New beginnings sometimes can or may happen unexpectedly. New beginnings are a forced shift of life that produce impromptu changes. They are a catalyst that gets the wheels rolling towards promoting change and growth in our lives. It starts with the process of shedding things. It's like all of sudden you start to downsize, getting rid of clutter, and/or making personal changes at a personal level. Shedding people, places, and even those close to us. It may even feel like a life crisis but it's not; it is often a preparation process. We have outgrown what we have gotten so used to. Therefore, we are pushed out of our comfort zone because if we stay, we lose ourselves by remaining mediocre. Have you seen the signs that they post when they are conducting the rehabilitation of a building? It usually states, "Under Construction." This means that you are in the preparation process. For example, it's like when you were growing up and you were used to a certain shoe size, and let's say that you needed a new pair, and you went to the shoe store. You keep trying on the same size you are so used to, and they don't fit anymore. You keep trying, thinking that maybe they are bringing you the wrong size, and you look at the shoe and see that it is the normal size you normally wear. The sales person comes in with the shoe measuring tool and says, "It looks like your feet have grown." You still believe that it's wrong. Why? Because conformity is like a habit that you are so used to and comfortable with. But you soon find out that you have outgrown the size and as a result the shoe feels uncomfortable, causes pain, and you can no longer walk comfortably in it. You may insist on continuing to wear the same size shoes, but you are going to be responsible for the consequences of the discomfort. Your stubbornness can keep you in the same spot if you become comfortable. The same holds true about life's shifts. All of a sudden you are no longer the same person you were so accustomed to being; you are different, you changed, and you no longer think the same way. You no longer fit in in your job, family, surroundings, or environment. Therefore, a shift is necessary in order to grow inside where it is most needed and then shift it outside to make the physical changes.

A new shift doesn't necessarily mean moving to another physical location unless that is something that you have been pondering on for a while. It could be as simple as moving to another city in your state or a new apartment or perhaps leaving a relationship, job, or changing career. The shift is not just one of a change in physical location only, but also it's an inside job flowing outwards. Everything must go, everything must change. Even the way you used to think. The shift will demonstrate a change in behaviors and the way you act, think, and associate with others. As a believer in Christ Jesus, we know that He has set a purpose and plan for our lives. And this plan is to prosper us and give us hope for a new future. We need to trust the process that God will be our provider, counsel, and guidance. We are to believe that with His divine guidance and leadership, we can do it. One of my favorite bible verses states, "I can do all things through Christ who strengthens me," Philippians 4:13. I have made this verse my daily self-affirmation.

Change and moving forward is not an easy decision and brings with it a sense of pain and uneasiness as well as discomfort. How do you leave what you are so used to? How do you separate yourself from what has become so normal and routine? How do you get the courage to leave the comfort of stagnation? Do you listen to the voice of God and allow Him to guide you? He can give you direction as to when is the right time to move. What do you do when you are in this place of restructuring? Are you willing to listen to His will? Remember that when God says go and He says leave everything, don't look back. You must listen to His still small voice whispering the direction and guidance. Yes, we must not look back. Don't do what Lot's wife did and be turned into a pillar of salt. This means that if you look back to the past, your spirit will remain in a place of stagnation with no growth. Becoming salty is just as bad as not having any flavor because you have outgrown things or been over seasoned.

In order to experience the breakthrough for which you have been waiting for so long, you must enter a period of isolation and purification. This process requires letting go of people, places, and things! It also involves leaving everything behind and sometimes going with just your clothes and luggage. Breathe for a second. I know that it is a hard thing to do, right? You see, the attachment to things can make you dependent on them and keep you in bondage. However, God is saying to you today, "I will make a way." "I will make everything new and give you more than you could ever imagine!" Can you trust what God is saying? You see, your mission and purpose is not attached to these things but to what is about to happen in your life. God will use it for His glory and for His kingdom. Get ready! The new season will bring new beginnings, new life, and new blessings. This will happen so that He can be glorified through your testimony, and His will be done through your life! We will begin to answer some questions to apply what we learned so far and start gaining insights into our lives in the next section.

Now, you can begin to apply what you have learned by answering these questions to the best of your knowledge, all while conducting self-introspection that will provide you with your sincere answers that will bring you clarification to where and how you stand in terms of becoming a life coach.

Questions

New Beginnings

1. Write down three things you can think of that you must let go of. Why do you think a new start would be healthy and productive for you? What does it look like to you? How prepared are you? If you are not, what would you need that can help become prepared? Do you feel that you are ready?

_____

_____

_____

_____

_____

_____

_____

_____

_____

_____

_____

_____

_____

_____

_____

Are you Prepared to Start a New Life?

"What does it take for us to start fresh and new? First, you must envision a life that you have always wanted or needed. How does it make you feel inside? What do you feel it will take for you to be convinced that this is what you are committed to do? Starting over is not easy for some people and requires risks, preparation, and action. What does it bring? Think of it like spring - there is something so very special about spring, the air is crisp, fresh, and clean. There is renewal by the sprouting of the flowers, their colors, and beauty. It provides us with a fresh sense of newness and appreciation of the old but still allows the new space to flourish. In the same way, we should embrace a new start in our lives." —Claribel Coreano

We have to admit that planning to make a change such as this can be intimidating. It is a super scary process making a spontaneous decision to start a new life. I know - I've been there! This is not driven by low-impulse control, no, not all. It is driven by a strong desire for change that is still backed up by calculated planning which does not offset your daily life but allows you to progressively take steps toward making the change. This is important because we often are not prepared or ready to take the plunge into a new beginning. We know that starting over brings new challenges, trials, and struggles. The anticipation can make you stall and not jump in the water while it's moving, waiting for the right time, or when you feel ready. This can or will affect your timing and cause deeper stagnation. We can never be fully prepared. There is a quote by Ashly Lorenzana that states, "The only thing that feels worse than being stuck in a situation that makes you unhappy is realizing that you are not ready or willing to change whatever it is."

During this process, we have to be extremely brave and bold to make those decisions. Think of it as if you are going away to college to prepare for your new future. After college you are on your way to a new you, career, or life. It's a preparation process we must embrace in order to grow. Before starting the planning, you must become organized, and this can be as simple as creating a timeline of your goals or creating a smart goal plan. Let's start by conducting an in-depth introspection of yourself, examining your weaknesses and strengths. You may start by asking yourself, "Am I ready for this?" Learning about yourself is important. Knowing your limitations, beliefs, or values that you possess as well as the ones that you need to work on or refine. This is the recommended inner work self-awareness and of course the first part of the process. Learning about yourself is important because you are entering a new phase of your life in which you must become totally vulnerable and conscious of who you are as a person. Once you do your own exploration, you will know more in depth about your strengths and weaknesses. This is necessary because you will be totally fully dependent on yourself to make the commitment to stay focused on your dreams. You have to be open to allow this process of refinement of your personality to take place so that you can become that highly successful business woman or man who you have dreamed of becoming.

Now, write down the areas in which you feel that you need to work on or refine. Next, take the necessary steps to work on those areas that need refinement. You may consider a life coach to help you keep focused and on track with your goals. If you need to take a course or attend a school to upgrade or fine-tune your skills, this is the perfect opportunity to do so. If you are going to start a business, I highly recommend a business life coach to help guide you step by step on how to execute your business plan if you're applying for a bank loan or other resources and support. It also will help you with setting up the financial structure of your business that will keep you in fidelity with all stakeholders. A business life coach can help you develop a financial plan of sustainability for your business for a projected 3–5 years. A business coach can help you develop a realistic budget to help you manage your business expenses, cost, payments, and income received. The business life coach will be instrumental in helping you acquire leads, learning how to lock clients into services, and bringing in steady income. If the coach is experienced in marketing, they may help you develop a marketing campaign to bring in clients. A business life coach is instrumental in teaching business management skills, teaching you different time management applications and other online apps that can best fit your business needs and help with time management. The good thing about having a business life coach is that they can teach you how to sell your services so that your business can grow financially.

Questions

Are you prepared to start a new life?

2. How can you start preparing yourself for this journey? Write down three things that you can think of that will help you with reaching a decision to start this new journey. What scares you the most? What do you look forward to the most? What are some things about yourself on which you must work?

_____

_____

_____

_____

_____

_____

_____

_____

_____

_____

_____

_____

_____

_____

_____

_____

The Preparation, Planning, and The Start of a New Journey

"Preparing, planning, and carrying out the start of a new journey is not as easy as we imagine it to be. It is a process like any other process that demands your attention, commitment, and action steps. First, the preparation is just the first part of the process which means that you are making yourself ready for this venture. The second step is the planning and thinking of how you are going to do this and how you are going to achieve this goal. Then the third is carrying out and taking action. It is those simple steps you start taking towards the goal of this new journey that takes you closer to the end goal."
—Claribel Coreano

Now, it's time for the outer work, which is the preparation, planning, and execution of starting this new journey. I always encourage planning ahead by organizing yourself in-house. This can be as easy as just simplifying your house or apartment. Simplifying yourself from any attachments or clutter is important. You may see it as having no purpose but it will help you get rid of things that you have less emotional attachments and no longer have use for or things you no longer need. Sometimes we keep items in our closets that we have bought but never used or will use but they just keep space in the closet. The same thing with household items, knickknacks, and other extra things that we keep as "just in case I need it." Another example is keeping christmas gifts in storage and not finding use for them. Unnecessary clutter takes up space and, according to Feng Shui experts, not only occupies space and energy but also creates stagnation. Keep in mind that this can be both in the physical and in the spiritual. You must ask God for discernment on spiritual refinement as it may mean losing relationships. If you are planning to move to a different location, start by making a list of the things that hold emotional value to you and prioritize them in order from most to least. Then, get rid of those things that you can do without, and keep the ones that you know that you cannot do without. Getting rid of things that you are no longer using or that you don't need is freeing. You can start simple by organizing your closet then moving from room to room. Box, label, and if anything is to be stored, label those boxes as well. Then, for anything that you have set apart for donations, start calling places that can accept donations or that can pick them up and set up a pickup schedule.

The next area of organization is your finances. Make sure that you have the financial resources to move to another city, state, or perhaps country. Create yourself a budget to start your journey into this new venture in life. Pay off debts and consolidate bills. Start saving more, eating out less, and cooking more at home. Planning meals, buying on sale, and thinking of other ways you can save. Adapting to being frugal can help when you are trying to do something that is going to change your life. It does not mean that you are cheap but that you are price conscious. Therefore, evaluate necessity versus price to stay living within your means. It is about becoming a more conscious buyer. And of course I am not suggesting to go without certain basic needs that you frequently use, not at all, but to become more price conscious, which allows you to free up some money to save. It is as simple as changing habits like that usual store-bought coffee that you normally buy each morning before work. For example, if you buy coffee each morning for $5.00 x 5 days is $25 per week, now that for 4 weeks each month $100 x 12 months is $1,200 which can save you towards your goal of planning your move. The same with eating out, if you normally eat 3 meals per week outside of the home, you are looking into big spending because it can add up to close to $50–$100 depending on the restaurant. Perhaps minimize eating out to either special occasions or one time per week, preferably the weekends. This is an adjustment that compensates you by saving money, and if you keep track of these types of expenditures you will feel proud of yourself when you count the amount of money you have saved. It is not just about being frugal but about being a smart shopper and conscious spender.

Create yourself a moving plan, looking for a certain neighborhood, school, location, or home. This will help you determine where you want to live, cost versus neighborhood, and many other things. Close all loose ends in your personal life, job, or with family. For example, obtain contact information for all medical providers, past references, networks, and families. Then, plan how you will start your search for employment, location, and preferred field. Revise your resume and update all of your references accordingly. Let them know that you will be relocating and that you will need their support. I highly encourage you to make a list every week to stay on task. Prioritize the tasks that you will need to complete and scratch off the items once completed. Make a list every week to keep you focused until you have reached your final day. Moving can be stressful, and I would also encourage creating a list once you move into the new location. Becoming organized, prepared, and disciplined makes everything run smoothly and fall into place much easier. If you have organized yourself prior to your move and made a list of everything you will need to do based on priority, you will find yourself adapting to the new location with ease and comfort instead of stressing about things you needed to do and may have overlooked. For example, if you have school-age children, make sure that you have all of their shots and school records ready to make their process easier to register in school. These are some skills that have worked for me in the past. I am sharing them just to incite some visual planning of what you will expect before and after. I am sure that many will have to develop their own style or process of organization, preparation, and planning. I encourage you to use what works for you as everyone has their own style of organization and tackling things. The important thing is to stay focused on the end goal - which is your growth. I would like to highlight that while you may not have to move or do this type of change, you will have clients that you will need coaching about this topic and will find this lesson helpful in guiding them with these changes and helping them to plan and evaluate if they are ready to make a change like this and what they will need to help them get started. Change is good but requires planning, preparation, and evaluation that it is indeed a positive change for the better for you. For example, if you go to 3 different interviews, you are not just going to take the first offer. No, you are going to want to hear from the other two to evaluate, which one is the most feasible for you that matches your skill set, culture norm of the company, and pay. In the very same way you must evaluate a decision to where to go, where to move, and when to make this change.

On the next pages, you will find some questions on the topic of starting a new life. Remember that many people talk about making changes like moving to another state or out of the country, but they are super afraid to take the risk and make these changes. These questions will help you to concentrate on how you would see yourself if you had to make this change in your life.

Questions

The Preparation, Planning, and The Start of a New Journey.

3. It is not an easy process as we might imagine it to be, however, it is a process that requires our focus. We must first prepare our mindset by conducting a thorough contemplation of what we would like to do and mapping out how we plan to do it. Lastly, taking the necessary action steps to move towards our goals. Can you think of a time in which you had to prepare yourself for an event, course, etc, that demanded preparation, planning and proactively taking action steps to ensure success? Write down an example of how you accomplish these three steps of preparation, planning, and action?

_____

_____

_____

_____

_____

_____

_____

_____

_____

_____

Starting New and Letting Go of the Old

There are two quotes that speak so clearly about new beginnings. The first one, "Every beginning comes from some other beginning's end."
—Seneca.

The second, "Never underestimate the power you have to take your life in a new direction." —Gregory Kent.

Both quotes share how new beginnings offer us the opportunity to have something new or go towards a new direction.

This new beginning requires a drastic change in the way you do things, speak, and make decisions. You are no longer the old you. You are a new person with an assigned new beginning. Wow, talk about self-discovery! A new beginning allows you to shed old habits and old ways of seeing and doing things that no longer fit or are working in your life. This process is extremely painful but necessary. It requires different phases, and the level of pain can be comparable to the process of eliminating certain things, people, places, and/or loved ones in order to free yourself to be able to move forward to being in the new. It is not an easy process because you must be willing to leave things or people behind that have deep-seated roots in your heart, thus creating discomfort. This is the shedding process. We all know that saying goodbye to people we love is painful, and it creates a question of "Did I do the right thing by leaving?" You can say that this process of shedding it is comparable to the stages of grief. There is denial, anger, bargaining, depression, and acceptance. The process often hits each person differently. Shedding the self is like shedding the ego; it requires a humbling experience to get you to look deep within yourself and find out who you truly are and what God has intended for you to do. This is the greatest discovery that a person can achieve, knowing that who they once were no longer exists, but what they are now is where they are supposed to be. It may have taken some time, but you now have achieved a better version of yourself.

Questions

Starting New and Letting Go of the Old

3. In preparation for this new journey, think of three habits you want to let go of. Write down how it will make you feel, letting these go, and how you would like to heal from it. Now, create three new habits with which you will substitute. Plan how you are going to address and prepare your loved ones for the newer version of you. What will be most helpful for you during this transition?

_____

_____

_____

_____

_____

_____

_____

_____

_____

_____

_____

_____

_____

_____

_____

_____

_____

_____

_____

_____

_____

_____

_____

_____

_____

_____

_____

_____

_____

_____

_____

_____

_____

_____

_____

_____

_____

_____

_____

Adjusting to the Vision of a New Life and Environment

"Adjusting to a new environment is not easy and can be uncomfortable. It's not easy because you will need to learn new things about your new surroundings and how they align with your vision, how to make it work to your benefit, and how to find the balance. Next is finding acceptance that can help you manage the new environment and your dreams at the same time. For example, it's like saying, 'Ok, I am here now,' and 'What do I do next? How can I make this work to my benefit?'" —Claribel Coreano

Adjusting your vision is to see that this new life and environment requires discipline, focus, and steady visual acuity in the present that will create the future for which you are hoping. How can we achieve this? First, we must stay grounded in God's word and in prayer. Placing everything in God's will and purpose and waiting on confirmation. While we wait, we must also continue to act and work towards our vision. We are not to stay stagnant without pushing forward as we must also push in prayer to see results and we must also place faith in action while we wait on God's approval. Hebrews 11:1, "Now faith is the assurance of things hoped for, the conviction of things not seen." In order to see the things that we hope for, we must put faith into action and imagine that we can see our vision manifesting in our lives. We must plan accordingly to see it happen. Writing it down in order to visualize it and bringing it to existence. Adjusting to the vision of a new life and a new environment takes some time to become fully acclimated to the new surroundings. One way you can do this is by preparing yourself to learn about the new environment.

Start preparing by researching the locations, businesses, networking opportunities, local churches, hospitals, and schools. Researching the new environment will help bring you ease and peace while determining if the decision you are making is a positive one. If you are a mom with school-age children, try getting connected with other moms from school or any online moms' group for support. Research what type of life coaching businesses are out there that can help you by possibly sharing their experiences or pointers on how to network or get clients once your business starts up. Connect and network with similar businesses to gather support and learn from their experiences. The new environment may bring its challenges but, as I mentioned in the prior paragraph, having an organized plan on how you plan to tackle the new environment will help lead you to the right people and positive connections. Building clientele is one of the hardest interactive action steps that you must take. You can network on different social platforms and other coaching sites. Social media platforms like Facebook offer many life coaching groups and marketing groups that share ideas and resources as well as opportunities to network together through podcasting, events, and workshops. Create your own elevator pitch or audio business card, as my coach calls it, on what services you provide, how they will help the client, and how you are going to coach them. This is needed to be used during community networking meetings and other events. For example, creating a free workshop at your local library may be a start or doing a pro-bono speaking engagement and other activities. You may also offer a 30-minutes or 1-hour free strategy coaching session to start engaging clients. You will know if you are ready to take on this challenge or not. The important thing is to try and continue to network until the right resources match you and what you offer. Another thing that you want to do is to seek a mentor, someone who will take you under their wings and share resources with you as well as get you acclimated to the new environment and people.

Questions

Adjusting to the Vision of a New Life and Environment

4. Write down how you plan to adjust your vision in order to become more disciplined and focused and think about how you see your future self. What steps are you willing to take to learn and rely on God's guidance and confirmation? How do you seek Him for guidance? Can you think of a time in which you depended on Him in which He came through for you? How did you feel? And what did you learn? Think of ways you are planning to tackle your new environment. Think of an area in which you feel that you will need the most guidance or need the most support. When you think of a mentor, think of how best will they be able to help you.

_____

_____

_____

_____

_____

_____

_____

_____

_____

_____

New Direction

"Are you asking God for direction before making a major decision? Exploring a new direction but only after receiving God's confirmation to act on it? This is needed to be able to have the peace and assurance that God will be with you throughout the Journey. Remember you are going to encounter many barriers or challenges. The important thing is not to become discouraged or give up. This is where you will need to depend on God, and on His divine guidance. This is something new that you are doing, and you are going to make mistakes, trials, and errors, but the important thing is to extract 'What did you learn from it? What can you do better next time? How can I become better empowered not to repeat the same mistake again?' By acknowledging what you have learned from these mistakes, you can use them for your benefit and for your growth as a tool." —Claribel Coreano

This new journey requires patience, self-control, and determination. You now have entered a new territory that you may not be fully familiar with, the things and cycles that you were used to are no longer available, and you will need to retrain yourself in certain processes. Know that you are bound to make mistakes, experience trials, and commit many unexpected errors. Throughout this whole experience, you may even have to repeat certain processes all over again. This is where you will need to evaluate what you learned from it. What can you do better next time to prevent you from repeating the same mistakes over again? As you practice, you will gain more knowledge and learn new skills with every tryout. Learning the resources that are available to you is important to help you navigate this new direction. While you are becoming more self-reliant and empowered, do not rely just on your own wisdom but seek to trust God in this process, no matter how difficult it becomes. "Trust in the Lord with your heart, and do not lean on your own understanding, in all your ways acknowledge him, and he will make straight your paths," Proverbs 3:5-6. This Bible verse is dear to me, and I hold it close to my heart. Why? Because we need to always make God our number one priority and our number one counsel by placing every decision that we are to make in his hands for confirmation and approval. Allowing for God to work in our lives, as He can direct our steps more clearly to avoid future disappointments. Always trust that He has our best interest in mind and will not lead us to a path of danger or destruction. Choose the right path! Consistent prayers are necessary, praying to God for direction and for His will for our life. God has a way of speaking to us as well as creatively giving us some signs.

During the time that I was contemplating this new transition to this new shift in my life, my eight-year-old granddaughter made me a paper fan with a poem written on it. She pleated it, and in each folded section, as part of the fan, she wrote something. I asked her to read it for me and this is what it said: "Choose the right path/As you have fun with your family and laugh/then you see the light of God shining bright/And you keep seeing it all through the night/ As you see the mighty angels saying you are free/And God won again as we say, 'Yes indeed'" God's answers are subtlety provided, always on time, and provide us with guidance. This simple poem not only proved that God was hearing my prayers but that He used my granddaughter to relay a beautiful message. From the mouths of babes, God speaks, and I understood the message in my heart. At that time, I was still debating on making a move towards a new life and had been experiencing a little bit of trepidation about the move. However, God spoke to me through her as if He were letting me know that I was free to move forward. My granddaughter also reassured me that it was ok to go, and that yes, she will miss me, but she looks forward to visiting me in my new location.

God used my granddaughter to provide me with confirmation that it was ok to leave and also say goodbye to her. She was ok with it because

God also gave her the comfort to accept this change was needed in my life as she had been extremely attached to me since she was a baby. It is important to learn how to evaluate when something is from God or not. Be careful because the way of the world may seem easy, comfortable, and enticing. Especially when you are struggling with making decisions on which path or which way to go, the enemy may try to sway you with distractions or try to keep you where you are at because it's comfortable. But no matter what, the enemy cannot distort the path where God is leading you to, but he will use many distractions to make you weary, second-guess yourself, or tempt you to change your mind. Remember, it's all about our own free will as nothing can be forced on us without God's permission. Choose the right path because the right path is where your blessings await you! The right path will open doors! The right path will set the foundation for your ministry. So, choose the right path today and do not sway! Remember, "God won again as we say yes indeed! You are free!"

Questions

New Direction Offers Clarity into a New Path

5. Before you make a decision, you need confirmation on what direction to go and where. How will you know if you are choosing the right path or not in life? Remember, discernment is important in making decisions. How will you know how to discern which path will be best for you? What do you need to feel comfortable that a decision you are making feels right?

_____

_____

_____

_____

_____

_____

_____

_____

_____

_____

_____

_____

_____

_____

_____

When You Are Thinking of a Career Change

"When thinking of a career change, you must evaluate what is needed and why. Evaluate your accomplishments and what you have achieved thus far. What have you contributed to the field or company? How can you now use that knowledge gained to a whole new level or in a new environment? How can you take all these skills to create a new job or business? Or perhaps use your expertise as a consultant. You must question, 'How is it going to benefit you in making this change?' Think of the pros and cons and new skills you can learn to complete the toolbox." —Claribel Coreano

There are times in our lives in which we become stagnant in a job or place and as a result will feel the need to move forward, especially when we have been working at a company for many years. In order for you to grow and learn new skills, you must move forward into a new environment.

- The first step to making a career change is to evaluate your skills, what you are passionate about, and what job will be your ideal job. Revamp and write down your weaknesses and strengths for this change and evolve as you grow. In addition, to evaluate salary, benefits, and location. You want to make sure that you will be happy at this new job or new career.

- Second, update your resume and cover letter to fit with the new objectives and start to visualize your ideal job. Taking a new course to upgrade your skills and become more competitive within the job market.

- Third, prepare yourself for this new change by mentally changing your mindset, thinking positively, and practicing what it would look like if you had your dream job.

- Fourth, practice interviewing skills, researching new trends, researching the company where you will be interviewed, and how to ask the right questions.

- Fifth, research and learn how to negotiate a salary. Sticking to your vision of the ideal salary but leaving room for negotiation.

- Sixth, send a thank-you note or email after an interview even if you feel it is an old school technique. There are many companies that still honor this practice. It is still common etiquette for Human Resources to highlight an applicant who sends a thank-you email or letter. It does not guarantee you the job but gets you noticed, so if you did very well during the interview and send a thank-you note, it will be highly noticeable.

- Seventh, if you do not get employed, you may want to ask the reasons as to why you were not hired. You can also ask that you want to receive positive feedback to help you with future interviews. Some companies are open to give feedback, others do not like to give feedback. It is a chance thing, but you never know if you don't ask. Some human resources companies will provide some information via email or mail letting you know that they have moved forward with another candidate, but others may not.

Even if you are a life coach, it is still empowering to conduct this process as you build your business. You may need to work to supplement income. Unless you are financially secure, you may just take the plunge right into your business start-up. Either way, taking new training that you will need for your business is essential, such as learning how to use Excel, marketing, and budgeting amongst many other business-related courses that can prepare you for this new venture of entrepreneurship. And remember that you most likely will need to help others in this area at one point or another throughout your coaching journey. So, make sure you document what worked and what did not work as a reference for future use. Every learning experience counts as a tool for your coaching toolbox. Career changes are not easy, and sometimes they come unexpectedly because of downsizing, new management, or business closures. Either way, being prepared is better than not being prepared. The following questions will help gear you towards the preparation part of the process. Start getting your thoughts in order by learning about your strengths and weaknesses as well as what your ideal career looks like, or even better, how you envision yourself as a life coach.

Questions

When You Are Thinking of a Career Change

6. Changing careers is not easy. You must evaluate the reasons why it will be beneficial for you versus staying and doing the same. What can you think of out of the top of your head that you do well and that also highlights your skills? What three positive things did you learn in your last job? What negative things affected your decision? If you could paint a picture of the perfect job, what would it look like?

_____

_____

_____

_____

_____

_____

_____

_____

_____

_____

_____

_____

_____

Sometimes a New Direction Requires that You Let Go of the Old

"Changing career paths can lead to new directions or changes in field as well as a change in location. The first thing is finding the paradigm of why it is needed. What's next? Letting go of the old so that you can embrace the new? How can you release yourself from the old? What steps can you take towards the new direction? What can you do to evaluate whether a career change is what you need or if staying in the same field will bring you contentment? Either way, it is time to plan, it is time to organize, it is time to evaluate, and it is time to make things happen towards the shift."

—Claribel Coreano

Changing the mindset of old thinking that "this is done this way" or "this is the way it's always been done" is important because you may soon find out that there are new ways to do the same exact things you did in your past job. Things change, the culture is different, and even human resources management is different from five years ago. The hiring process is completely different from 10–15 years ago. Now, everything is conducted online from the application process to time keeping, check deposits, and administering training and is done through many different employment search engines and apps. There have been many changes to accommodate new human resources laws regarding leave of absence, parents' leave, special accommodation, workplace bullying, risks management, and many other special interest policies. The same holds true on letting go of people, places, and things. While it may sting for a minute, you will become home sick and miss the old, but know that God's plan is always the best plan for our life. God has a plan and a purpose for your life. "For I know the plans I have for you, declares the Lord, plans to prosper you and not to harm you, plans to give you hope and a future," Jeremiah 29:11. When God gives you a vision, what do you do with it? What determines what you are led to do? How ready do you need to be? How equipped do you feel? If God has a plan and a purpose for your life, why doubt that He will make sure that things will be for your own good? You know deep in your heart and soul that there is a greater calling for your life, but the enemy has smeared your life with poisonous lies. The enemy knows what God is trying to do in your life and has his own plan and vision to divert you from God's original purpose for your life. You see, if he is successful, he will totally destroy your life with sin, distraction, and entice you to do worldly things.

What do we do when God gives us a vision? We must come to Him in all humbleness and surrender and ask Him, "What do you want from my life and how do you want to use me?" You may already have an inkling of what it is, but you want His affirming confirmation that this is His will for your life. What determines where you will be led to do is the fact that it should be done to always glorify His holy name! Then, you must fight for it and work towards taking the steps of actions to get it done! God can provide you with a map or blueprints but, if you are not obedient to His instructions, you will be like the Israelites and be lost in the desert for 40 years! How ready do you need to be? How equipped do you feel? The most effective people in the Bible were ordained, called impromptu, chosen, and anointed with no knowledge of what exactly they were going to do or how they would be used. You see, that is where the Holy Spirit comes in. He is the voice that will inspire and speak what needs to be said. We think that in order for God to use us, we need to be perfect, speak elaborately, or be ready. This is not true as God speaks through the meek, uses the radical, eccentric, or weird to voice messages that glorify His name. So, what are you doing with the vision God has given you? What has been stopping you? What do you need to do to move forward and make it happen? In the next pages, you will explore some questions that will help you evaluate the direction and search within for answers to where God is calling you too.

Questions

Sometimes a New Direction Requires that You Let Go of the Old

7. It is difficult getting rid of the old because we become so attached to it. What do you need to let go of? What carries the most weight and often weighs you down? Who do you have to let go of and who do you have to forgive? Have you evaluated the direction God is calling you to? What are you doing with the vision God has given you? What has been stopping you? What do you need to do to move forward and make it happen?

_____

_____

_____

_____

_____

_____

_____

_____

_____

_____

_____

_____

_____

Why Does the Old Way Not Work for You Anymore?

The old becomes a baggage of heaviness, doubts, and/or barriers, a negative mindset towards where you are being led too. It creates fears of leaving the old ways that you are accustomed to doing things. You can become stagnant because you feel comfortable or relaxed because you already know the routine. But it doesn't work anymore for you. Deepak Chopra states in one of his quotes, "In the process of letting go you will lose many things from the past, but you will find yourself." There is another beautiful quote about letting go by Jeffrey McDaniel that states, "I realize there's something incredibly honest about trees in the winter, how they're experts at letting things go."

The old does not fit anymore, like the analogy of the outgrown shoe that I provided in an earlier chapter. God wants to use you at a different level, in a different manner, and in a different environment so that His name can be glorified. We can't grow personally, spiritually, or professionally if we stay with the old. Old things depreciate in value. Therefore, the old ways of doing things or thinking no longer serve a purpose in your life. In order to achieve the vision or plan that God has for you, we must be able to let go of the old. It's a painful process but we must let go of the familiar things, people, jobs, family, and/or location.

Letting go will make you feel like a weight has been lifted, and you become more focused or disciplined in your vision. The new requires stepping out into a bold stance of courage to accept the new challenges that it may bring. The new requires you to get out of the box of conformity and learn to become empowered in the areas in which you are lacking. Now, it's the time to learn what you are really made of. You are capable of doing great things if you step out of your comfort zone.

There is a quote by Roy T. Bennett that says, "You never change your life until you step out of your comfort zone; change begins at the end of your comfort zone." Another quote by Bennett talks about change being difficult and goes like this: "Real change is difficult at the beginning. But gorgeous at the end. Change begins the moment you get the courage and step outside your comfort zone; change begins at the end of your comfort zone.

Getting out of your comfort zone requires getting rid of things in you that weigh you down like past baggage, resentment, negative mindsets, distorted self-image, anger, or vengeance and many other things that may be causing you to stay stagnant.

Pay attention to any feelings of doubt or fear and barriers that need to be tackled right away before you go into your role of a life coach. For example, let's say that you are a bottle, and inside the bottle, it has been filled with all the negative things of the past: fears, doubts, etc. Change happens and requires the bottle to be emptied in order to add the new skills, new mindset, positivity, and commitment amongst many other positive traits. Be careful what you add to your bottle as it is fragile and valuable. Preserve yourself from toxicity, negativity, and unsafe environments. In the next page, you will answer some questions that will help you self-reflect on anything that is holding you down that must be brought to the surface and addressed and then discarded. This process allows you to have room for a new, more productive way of living.

Questions

Why Does the Old Way Not Work for You Anymore?

8. What baggage from the past do you carry? What doubts, fears, and barriers have created obstacles in you in accomplishing your dreams? Name them, face them, address them, and think of ways that you can get rid of them. What can you change in you that can help you get rid of all the things that are no longer working for you?

_____

_____

_____

_____

_____

_____

_____

_____

_____

_____

_____

_____

_____

_____

_____

New vs. Old - Evaluating the Pros and Cons.

"In order to appreciate the new and see the difference it brings, you must be prepared to compare and contrast it to the old. This process can be implemented during the phase of exploration by writing down the benefits of what you hope to accomplish and any negative sidelines, barriers, or obstacles that you may experience. This preparation is so that you know how to prepare yourself for the challenges without becoming a surprise. Not to say that we must not go through or experience some barriers; no, sometimes this type of experience becomes a propelling catalyst that will help you work harder. It also will help you determine how you can make it work the next time, any pitfalls to avoid, and what worked or did not work during the process. This will also help you notice the difference between the old and the new way of things." —Claribel Coreano

The new brings a surge of energy and passion. You will feel focused, motivated, and disciplined to work on your own vision. The new offers a new direction, a new way of doing things, new behaviors, and new purpose. The new will bring success in different ways whether it is financially, health-wise, or through new relationships. The old may feel corroded as nothing is improving or allowing progress to take place. The old may be familiar; however, it can make you feel drained or unmotivated if it no longer creates a spark in your life. Also, the old keeps you stuck in a nonproductive mindset. Let go of the old. There is a quote by Lauren DeEstefano that states, "Set fire to the broken pieces; start anew." In the very same way we should think of the old, to be able to visualize it diminishing so that it allows room for the new.

How can you reach the point of realization that the old is no longer working? And how can you visualize and manifest the new? Here are some tips to consider:

- First, make a list of the things that are no longer working in your life and why.

- Second, ask yourself what must I do to change these things that no longer work for me?

- Third, ask yourself how can I replace them with something new?

- Fourth, list action steps on how you are going to replace them with what you want to manifest in your life. Whether it is a change of relationship, location, work or habits, and things that no longer bring you joy that act as barriers in your lives because it keeps you stagnant.

- Fifth, make sure that you set a goal with target dates for the things you want to manifest and the things you want to get rid off. In this way you will hold yourself accountable and committed to take action.

You can find out more of this can create positive change in your life by conducting an evaluation of both the old and the new, and how it will benefit you the most. Remember, conformity is habit forming, and when you are used to doing something for such a long time, it becomes so easy, routine, and habitual. This is a hard wall to break through. You must accept what staying with the old brings to you. Does it bring you comfort? Security? Stability? These are great but can become boring with time. Sometimes, a shake out of the box of conformity and out of the habitual can bring you an exciting freedom. This freedom cannot be found in the old. The new will bring you everything and then some, more so than you ever had in the old. In due time there will be added blessings because you are walking into your purpose or ministry God designed for you. It will bring you contentment and joy. Even when you are going through difficulties, God will show up and provide you with comfort and joy. In addition, it will bring more growth in every aspect of your life, whether physically, spiritually, financially, or mentally. It's worth getting rid of the old to bring in the new of God's blessings. In the next page, you will be able to explore some questions that will help you in learning what is keeping you holding onto the old and what you need to do to embrace the new.

Questions

New vs. Old - Evaluating the Pros and Cons

9. Now that you know yourself better, write down the benefits of what you hope to accomplish by embracing the new. Write down what you hope to accomplish getting rid of the old. Evaluate any negative sidelines, barriers, or obstacles that you may experience during this process of shedding. Write down how you feel knowing what you will look forward to getting rid of old ways vs. new ways of doing things.

_____

_____

_____

_____

_____

_____

_____

_____

_____

_____

_____

_____

_____

_____

_____

_____

_____

_____

_____

_____

_____

_____

_____

_____

_____

_____

_____

_____

_____

_____

_____

_____

_____

_____

_____

_____

God's Will and His Timing

Why is asking God for His will and timing for our plans important? I have learned from experience to respect that God has given us free will to learn those lessons about timing. We precipitate into action, trying to rush the process, when in fact God wants us to take our time in order to learn some lessons or how to become more experienced and gain more maturity that will be needed to exercise the vision. He knows, He sees, He listens, and He witnesses our past, present, and future and what will work or not. That's intense, but He is the ultimate compass that we should be relying on for timing. There is a quote by Eddie Huang that goes like this: "People talk about perfect timing, but I think everything is perfect in its moment; you just want to capture that."

In Psalm 27:14, "Wait for the Lord; be strong and take heart and wait for the Lord." This Bible verse encourages us to stay strong, which means to stay confident, expecting that for which you are hoping. And during the waiting period, take heart - which means to stay with good intentions and hope that, whatever we are waiting upon the Lord to do, will come to pass in His own timing. It is important to put all of your plans and dreams in God's hands through prayers and supplication. Fasting and placing God first in every decision and everything you do. Honoring Him, His will, and His timing. Another Bible verse that speaks on waiting on His timing, "He has made everything beautiful in its time. He has also set eternity in the human heart; yet no one can fathom what God has done from beginning to end," Ecclesiastes 3:11. There is a guarantee that comes with this verse and that is what God does is always wholesome and beautiful, and He makes it this way in His timing. His will for us is always going to lead us to the right path, and it will be a blessing. There is a quote by G. Campbell Morgan that goes like this: "Waiting for God means power to do nothing save under command. This is not a lack of power to do anything. Waiting for God needs strength rather than weakness. It is the power to do nothing. It is the strength that holds strength in check. It is the strength that prevents the blundering activity which is entirely false and will make true activity impossible when the definite command comes." We have to be careful not to act before the appointed time as it will cause delays or hardships and may not come out beautiful as He intended because we put our two cents in to rush it. God knows the Kairos time that will lead to doors opening and blessings. Sometimes, when we do our own and not allow God to work on our lives, it actually delays the process because we intervene. As a result, we will need to begin again, now with lessons learned. Have you ever done this? Or have you ever realized yourself becoming inpatient because it's taking too long? How can you rely on God to pull through instead of your own will? What do you need to do to allow God to take the wheel? The following questions will help you reflect on God's timing and how you can be patient during the process while still anticipating success.

Questions

God's Will and His Timing

10. How will you know God's timing? How will it help you choose right? Can you write one sentence based on what you envision? You may feel like it's taking too long - how can you rely on God to pull through instead of your own will? What do you need to do to allow God to take the wheel?

_____

_____

_____

_____

_____

_____

_____

_____

_____

_____

_____

_____

_____

_____

_____

_____

_____

_____

_____

_____

_____

_____

_____

_____

_____

_____

_____

_____

_____

_____

_____

_____

_____

_____

_____

_____

_____

_____

_____

Confirmation and Guidance

"Why is seeking guidance and confirmation important? First and foremost, guidance and confirmation should be coming directly from God. Yes, of course, God may use someone with a prophetic voice to confirm some things relating to what God is doing in your life, but your main confirmation is through His word and through prayer. And remember, just like God sends confirmation, the enemy also sends its own agents disguised as light to distort God's plan for your life and cause confusion or delays. Be alert and sober-minded to know a counterfeit from a godly person." —Claribel Coreano

So far, throughout this book, we learned that God should be priority and that He gives us the confirmation to either proceed or start over. He is the ultimate, trustworthy entity that will not lead us into anything that will bring us pain and suffering. One way that you can obtain direction and clarity is through prayers and staying in the word. There is a quote by E.M. Bounds which states, "The goal of prayer is the ear of God, a goal that can only be reached by patient and continued and continuous waiting upon Him, pouring out our heart to Him and permitting Him to speak to us. Only by doing so can we expect to know Him, and as we come to know Him better we shall spend more time in His presence and find that presence a constant and ever-increasing delight." This means having the trust that He is working everything for your good even during the waiting period. The next step that you can take towards obtaining confirmation is to seek mentorship, advice from church elders, or expertise from someone who you know has experience in something that you are struggling with. They do not come to do the work for you or give it to you, but instead to show you or teach you how to do it. They can be the resounding voice of paraphrasing that will help you look within for your own answers. That's how impactful these interactions can become; therefore, these are chosen and anointed people who God uses in a mighty way. They will know that it is you who they need to support. These often come through divine appointments or visions. God confirms it to them as well. I have met a few angels like that in my lifetime. I am here to tell you that they do exist, and God uses these people to bring confirmation.

In 1st Timothy 3:1, "Here is a trustworthy saying: Whoever aspires to be an overseer desires a noble task." Get confirmation from elders, mentors, and through prayers that it is the will of God for your life. God knows what you will need in your journey and any obstacles that you may encounter that will need the support of kingdom believers' prayers to help you stay on track. Therefore, it is always a promising idea to consult with a godly person who has a history of prayer and godly wisdom. This person will have a good moral character and will be able to have strong discernment to assist you in guiding you to the right path. Prayers and mentorship are necessary because sometimes we may find ourselves so busy with getting things done that we rush or become overwhelmed and do not see things objectively.

Just remember that although there is confirmation, it does not mean you are immune from experiencing hardships or delays. In fact, you may experience more attacks in your life than before because you are working toward your purpose. These delays or barriers come in the form of people, places, resources, finances, and emotional or physical health. In Nehemiah's 4:1-4 provides us with an excellent example that when we start to work on our purpose or God's plans for our lives; we are to expect opposition both from within our most closest circle (which is family) and external circles (which are friends, acquaintances, and even strangers who may know of us, but we don't know of them). The enemy uses people, places, and things to attempt to distort God's plan for our lives. We need to pay close attention to those things and use discernment. We will find that people out of nowhere will slowly disengage from our lives. People who you thought would support you will not and are now basically mocking your efforts and progress. Verse 1 states, "When Sanballat heard that we were rebuilding the wall, he became angry and was greatly incensed." He ridiculed the Jews, and in the presence of his associates and the army of Samaria, he said, "What are those feeble Jews, doing? Will they restore their wall? Will they offer sacrifices? Will they finish in a day? Can they bring the stones back to life from those heaps of rubble—burned as they are?" You can sense the tone and mockery from what they were saying about their efforts. They were openly mocking Nehemiah's determination to build the wall, not because they themselves wanted to build it or felt that they could build it, but because it was Nehemiah's purpose. He stood out in front of them as a person of integrity and of his word. Nehemiah placed his trust and faith in God throughout the whole process, he maintained himself in peace and stayed focused on what God told him to do.

On the other hand, his enemies saw no hope in them rebuilding the wall nor were they supportive of Nehemiah. But Nehemiah saw beyond what they could visibly see, he envisioned it like God allowed him to dream it, and he saw it as a finished project. Like Nehemiah, you will experience mockery, jealousy, and rejection from some people. This is where you need to stand strong in the word of God and in prayers. You will also have to sacrifice relationships, a job, or face distancing yourself from people who do not believe in your dreams. This is, in fact, important to realize - that what God is doing in your life is so big that He desires for no one else to take the glory for what He is doing. He doesn't want anyone else taking the credit for all the miracles that He intends to do in your life. He deserves the glory as He is working in your life to help you become the person that you have been designed to be by Him. He will use you for His kingdom; you just have to trust the process throughout all the opposition and rejection. I can testify that it is indeed a lonely place to be and that you will experience many challenges but, at the end of it all, you will also experience victory because you will start to see the vision become alive. The next page you will explore some questions that will help you to recognize when you need to wait on God or obtain confirmation from Him and others.

Questions

Confirmation and Guidance

11. Why is seeking mentoring and confirmation important? Do you feel that God has given you confirmation to move forward with your goals? If so, how do you know? What confirmation have you received? How will you handle the mockers, the naysayers, and those who do not celebrate your progress?

_____

_____

_____

_____

_____

_____

_____

_____

_____

_____

_____

_____

_____

_____

_____

The Vision

Why do you need a vision? A vision is like a road map that you design for yourself to follow a goal, ministry, or dream that you want to fulfill. It helps you set a detailed written plan of things that you want to accomplish and what you hope it will bring forth. It will keep you accountable to follow it and fulfill the purpose. However, it may change as the goal progresses or solidify once you have built a foundation for it and the business or ministry is thriving. "Make your vision so clear that your fears become irrelevant." —Anonymous

The word of God tells us in Psalm 37:4, "Delight yourself also in the Lord, and He shall give you the desires of your heart." This Bible verse encourages us to seek God first and ask what we need or want for our lives. He will give us the desires of our heart as long as they align with His will and purpose for our lives. It doesn't mean that we should just wait to see if it falls in our lap, no, not all. It means to be expectant of it with hope about what you have not yet seen but believing that God will come through for you. So, what is a vision? A vision is a manifestation of what you want to see or be accomplished in the future. It is also a work plan that you can use to set your guidance on future actions. It delineates all your core values of what your business represents, what it hopes to accomplish, and the outcome or result of how it will help others. In addition, your vision also directs what actions you need to take towards accomplishing the vision.

According to the Merriam-Webster dictionary, a vision is defined as, "the act or power of seeing and mode of seeing or conceiving." Having a vision is like having a compass that determines the direction you must go. The vision is a road map of what you see to be fulfilled via this vision, what you want to do, how you will do it, what steps you will take to do it, and what will be the expected outcome of why you want to do it. How do you envision yourself in this new beginning? Can you visualize what you are expecting? Can you feel it, see it, and yearn for it? Is there passion behind the struggles to make it happen? You know when something is going to be blessed by God because everything and anything negative starts to happen. We often perceive that if it is from God then we will not experience any challenges or that it will be smooth sailing.

That is not necessarily the case and, in fact, there is a saying that goes like this: "The higher the calling, the more the enemy attacks." Obstacles become apparent for no reason, and you will experience some form of stagnation that can only be removed through prayers. You have to keep pushing for this new beginning. Proverbs 16:3 states, "Commit your works to the Lord and your plans will be established." This verse firmly encourages us to place God first by committing all of our plans in His hands. It is necessary for us to also understand that our plans may not be God's plans for our lives at that particular moment or the timing may not be the best. He knows if something is not yet ready or if perhaps there is a task that He desires for you to complete before the blessings are fulfilled. And, like the verse in Habakuk states, "Though it tarries, wait for it will surely come." Therefore, we need to ask for His guidance and His will for our lives. Even during the time of waiting, we must still be expecting our breakthrough. In Psalm 37:5, it clearly encourages us that we need to "commit your way to the Lord, trust also In Him, and He will do it." The word "commit" is a reminder that we need to establish that we are ready for this challenge. This means that we must become proactive and take actions towards the execution of the plan. We must have a firm faith and believe that with His guidance we can accomplish it all. James 1:5, "If any of you lacks wisdom, you should ask God, who gives generously to all without finding fault, and it will be given to you." This means that God wants for us to ask Him for wisdom, clarity, and discernment when we are not sure of how to proceed. We must trust that He has everything under His control and that He wants for us to keep having faith in His provision and blessings for our lives. The following questions will help you start thinking about creating and visualizing your vision.

Questions

The Vision

12. Write down a statement of your vision. What do you see? How will you accomplish it? What will you need? How will it represent you or your business? Does it highlight your values? Does it speak your language, and what do you hope to achieve? Will you be open to receive God's guidance and follow His direction?

_____

_____

_____

_____

_____

_____

_____

_____

_____

_____

_____

_____

_____

_____

Mission

Why do you need a mission? "Where there is no revelation, people cast off restraint, but blessed is the one who heeds wisdom's instruction," Proverbs 29:18. Just like a vision, a mission is just as important in voicing what you intend to accomplish in a more refined, detailed, clarified, and concise language that speaks not only of your vision but your brand, business, or ministry. "To succeed in your mission, you must have a single-minded devotion to your goal." —Abdul Kalam

The Merriam-Webster dictionary defines "mission" as, "a specific task with which a person or a group is charged," or "a pre-established and often self-imposed objective or purpose." So, you created your vision. What is your purpose, what will you be doing, and how do you intend to complete it? Creating and writing down a mission is just as important as your vision. The mission clarifies the vision, the purpose of what you are going to be doing, and how you intend to carry it out and why. Write it down, every detail, and revise it until you feel like it can be your branding. For anyone who wants to complete a goal, create a vision or mission. You must first obtain clarity and explore areas that you will need to experience growth in. The first thing you must do is to create the goal you want to accomplish by writing a statement about what you want to do or accomplish as well as how and why you want to do this. You will then explain what will be expected or the outcome you expect to achieve from this goal by first creating a vision statement. How you see what you are going to do, how it will benefit others or provide a service for others. In Habakkuk 2:3, "For the vision is yet for an appointed time, but at the end it will speak, and it will not lie, though it, tarries wait for it because he will surely come, it will not tarry."

First you must learn about yourself before servicing others to better understand where God is directing you to. This is important so that you will know what areas of ministry or population that He wants you to serve. Another thing you must do is to explore your gifts because there may be some gifts that you have not yet brought to the surface that can be used for the kingdom, ministry, or business. How will you serve others with these gifts? God has blessed you with these gifts to best serve Him and others. Now, the next step is to learn and explore any areas in which you are proficient. Explore what challenges you are facing and do a thorough and complete introspection of yourself to identify any barriers, obstacles, or areas in which you tend to sabotage yourself in. Learn to love yourself before serving others. Always practicing self-care because you cannot serve others on an empty cup. It has to be overflowing so that you can share what is outpouring out of you.

The most important thing to do is an emotional check up by identifying any triggers in your temperament so you can learn how to manage and regulate it before it controls you. As you will experience many difficult situations in which you may feel hot and bothered by people, situations, or personal attacks. Many people think that anger may be the problem when it is really your temperament that may be the one out of control. Let's clarify what temperament is; if you have the temperament of becoming impulsively angry frequently, you are acting on a learned behavior that is instinctively demonstrating anger. This temperament is a learned behavior that can be associated with upbringing, values, or attitudes. Therefore, there is room to learn how to control, manage, and change the behavior. Now, reacting in anger is when the person has associated the anger as a self-defense mechanism. Anger, like any other emotion, is a healthy part of human emotions. What is toxic is the way a person reacts in anger rather than acting in response to the emotion of anger and managing it effectively. You must first learn how to manage that area of your life in order to regulate your emotions because you will be challenged and tested by situations as well as others. Now comes the good part - and the most challenging one. The following questions will help you learn more about yourself and how to manage and regulate your anger or temperament, trigger, and also help change your mindset. These reflective questions can help you dig deep within so that you find your own answers to these situations and become self-aware of your own deficiencies in order to turn them into strengths and create inner growth.

You must ask yourself the following:

1. What will it take to get me where I need to be?
2. How can I change my mindset?
3. How can I become more focused?
4. How can I control any ruminating thoughts of self-defeat?
5. How can I combat negative thinking patterns?
6. How can I create a skill that will help me prevent any triggers?
7. How can I manage and regulate my anger or temperament during difficult situations or challenges?
8. How can I stay focused on the end goal without allowing any distractions to divert the tasks?
9. How can I practice self-care daily to help manage stress and balance my work and family life?
10. How can I best show up for my clients?
11. What do I need to do to help me stay grounded prior and after any life coaching sessions?
12. What can I adopt as a mantra or affirmation to remind me on how to stay focused, motivated, and passionate about what I do? (This can be a quote, an affirmation, or Bible verse.)

Creating your own self-soothing, affirmative or grounding exercises to help you stay present and let go of all distractions prior to meeting with a client or addressing a situation. This will also assist you to help your client stay grounded prior to a session. Let's say they come to their session and you notice that they look stressed and aspirated. Rather than going into the session right away, ask them, "How was your day?" or "How are you?" Part of engagement is to allow them to have an opportunity to share on how bad or good their day was or how stressful. If they keep it to themselves it will distract them from the session. And although what they disclose may not necessarily have to do with their goals, it will allow the client to feel validated and heard. Afterwards, it is good practice to be guided with a grounding or a relaxation exercise that can help the client become present in the moment and be able to benefit from the session. Again, it can be as simple as guided imagery exercise, affirmation, or you can even ask the client, "What will help you become more present and feel more relaxed?" The person can be worried about the day or stressed or has a lot on his or her mind. As a result, their mind will feel cluttered, and they will not be receptive to finding their own answers as their mind will be too preoccupied with other things. Therefore, adapting to this practice helps get them back into the coaching mode.

It's important to identify any areas that you are struggling with and give it a name. For example, a lack of focus causes chaos. Psychologists suggest that if your house, room, or car are messy, cluttered, or disorganized, so are your thought processes. Cleaning up clutter physically and mentally will help you stay focused and on track. Challenge question: How can you create more of what will help you become more focused? You have identified all of these areas and conducted a thorough introspection of yourself; you have identified barriers, areas of concern, challenges, and opportunities. Now it's time to take action. For example, stating, "I will work on myself to become more focused by creating a goal plan, setting a weekly schedule or daily task list. I will work on myself in creating a healthier mindset by focusing on the positive thoughts, catching myself when I have stinky thinking, and focusing on positives rather than negative outcomes." You are getting closer to progress. What small step are you willing to take today to move forward toward your purpose? And lastly, don't forget to pray and ask God for direction as well as confirmation that you are on the right track or heading toward His will and purpose for your life. Stephen Covey states, "Creating and integrating an empowering personal mission statement is one of the most important investments we can make." Think of this quote and start by creating an empowering personal mission statement that will help you stay focused. Are you ready to take on this challenge? Let's get started!

Questions

Mission

13. Write down your mission statement. The mission statement is more specific than your vision statement. Therefore, you will need more time to think about it and develop it. You may start by forming a paragraph that clarifies your vision, then the purpose of what you intend to do, what you are going to be doing, how you intend to do it, and any possible outcomes of it. What small step are you willing to take today to move forward towards your purpose? Think big, think greatness, as it will help to become more inspiring. Now, start brainstorming by writing three sentences that will help you get started with your mission. Then, move forward with writing a paragraph. Once you develop this paragraph, review, and revise it until you are convinced that this is it - it represents your business and matches with the branding that you are envisioning with.

_____

_____

_____

_____

_____

_____

_____

_____

_____

Dream of the Dream

Ephesians 3:16-17, "I pray that out of his glorious riches he may strengthen you with power through his Spirit in your inner being, So that Christ may dwell in your hearts through faith. And I pray that you, being rooted and established in love." It's such a great feeling to speak about your dreams or what you are hoping to accomplish in life. However, keep your dreams safe as they are not to be shared with just anyone until you have finalized them or have established your business. Unless you are working with a business coach or marketing coach and financial advisor. These are the people you should be discussing your plans with; otherwise, stay silent until you are fully operating in your calling. Also, remember that these are personal goals that you must bring to the Lord first in order to become strong spiritually to better handle challenges and to stay grounded when God gives you what you want. Always remember that once you achieve them, you can share your dreams with the world so that His name can be glorified by it. —Claribel Coreano

When working on your goals, you have to have a set of clear values that will set a standard for you to follow. This is necessary so that you will be able to develop a strategy that will not only help guide you but also keep you on task with following your dreams. It is imperative to maintain your commitment and focus. To do this you must first create an action plan with tasks and target deadlines. The action plan will serve as a task manager that will assist you in keeping focused on each individual goal, tasks, and taking action to complete it within a time frame. Action plans are super helpful whenever you want to complete a project or tasks as it details each action in order of priority, what will be needed, who will do it, and the time limit for completion of each task. Below are some task descriptions that should be included in the plan:

1. Create an action or business plan.
2. Create your mission and vision statement.
3. Execute the plan, live the mission and vision.
4. Seek resources, network, and find support when needed.
5. Keep track of all action steps completed, unfinished business, and other new revised additions to the plan.
6. Revise and update as needed, preferably by noting completed, pending, or revised with a date of completion.

To start putting what we have learned to practice, the next page will allow you to brainstorm on three goals to develop with action steps needed to achieve them.

Questions

Dream of the Dream

14. Now we get to work to become organized and focused by detailing what you want to achieve on paper, describing tasks, action, resources, and other specific things that you will need for your business. Name three goals you desire to achieve. Write a statement as to how you plan to achieve them, what you will need, how you will tackle them, and what you hope to accomplish. Remember that "A dream doesn't become reality through magic; it takes sweat, determination, and hard work." - Colin Powell

What do you think about this quote? And why? Dreams have to be written on paper in order to manifest them.

_____

_____

_____

_____

_____

_____

_____

_____

_____

_____

_____

_____

Example of an Action Plan

In life or business, you need to set goals and create an action plan in order to be successful. There is a quote by Pooja Agnihotri that states, "A strategy is an action plan of what you want to achieve and how. It defines where you want to see yourself in the long-term and how you are going to use your resources, skills, and competencies to achieve that." And one way that you can do this is by creating an action plan to help guide you in the process. Here is an example of an action plan that I have created in this easy-to-follow format just to give you an idea on how you can break it down. First, you must break down priority through numbering, and then a short sentence describing the goal, a short statement of the goals itself, or an objective description of the goal that includes action-oriented language that you can include in your action plan. You will then break down the task and how you plan to achieve it. While you are working on your dreams, you also want to work on creating, finding, and maintaining balance in your life in all areas. Especially all the areas of your life that need restructuring, growth, and/or change. Action plans are an excellent tool that will help you to complete your goals and achieve your dreams. The following page will provide you with a detailed example of an action plan that will help you learn how to structure your goals and set realistic goals with target dates and detailed tasks. This is the fun part where you get to visualize your goals and objectives in order to stay on track and be successful in accomplishing your goals.

Personal Goals for _____ Year: daily review of goals

Goal 1: Spirituality- "I want to improve my relationship and walk with God"

I would like to become closer to God by increasing prayers and reading the Bible. Second, I want to share what God has done in my life. Third,

I want to work on myself by restraining myself from speaking any unwholesome speech, rejecting any negative thoughts, and working on becoming a better person daily.

Daily and weekly goals start on _____.

1. Pray daily morning and evening.
2. Read the Bible daily morning and evening.
3. Write in a journal what I learned from each Bible chapter.
4. Share with others when prompted by the Holy Spirit.
5. Refrain from speaking negative words daily practice.
6. Be mindful of my thoughts daily practices.
7. Forgive more daily practice.
8. Fasting once or twice a month.

Goal 2: Business- "I want to launch my coaching business by spring _____ (Date/Month/Year)"

I would like to work on launching my business this year on _____(date/month/year).

I aim to create change, expect growth, achieve happiness, create abundance, obtain healing, and restoration!! I will work on all necessary steps in order to achieve a successful end goal of creating my own business.

Work on life coaching business start-up by: _____.

1. Life coach certification by: _____.
2. Obtain an LLC by _____.
3. New website to be completed by: _____.
4. Create new cards by: _____.
5. Create branding/logo and brochures by: _____.
6. Get three clients by: _____.
7. Conduct a free workshop by: _____.

8. Manage social media: _____.
9. Publish new materials podcast by:_____.
10. Weekly blogs by: _____.
11. Complete all coaching forms by: _____.
12. Manage marketing to increase clients engagement by: _____.

Completion Date: _____.

Goal 3: Personal Care- "I want to take better care of myself and improve my overall health & wellbeing."

Self-care is important; I am first and need to care for my health and my wellbeing. "I can't pour an empty cup; I need for my cup to overflow to impart from my outpouring to others."

I would like to start working on my self-care by _____ with a monthly review of my goals at the end of each month.

Organize myself:

1. Create a task list or follow a task manager app (like Toggl or Friday) to stay focused, motivated, and committed daily.

    Start date:_____

2. Follow an appointment schedule and planner.
3. Limit idle time.
4. Monitor social media, no TV or social media before bedtime.

    Completion Date: _____.

Boundaries:

1. Write down things that you make feel uncomfortable or that you notice that you overextend yourself.
    Implement by _____
2. Write down your list of boundaries for work life

Implement by _____

3. Write down your list of boundaries for personal life
   Implement by _____
4. Write down your list of boundaries for relationship
   Implement by _____
5. Write down your list of boundaries for family
   Implement by _____
6. Write down your list of set boundaries on; learning when to say yes and when to say "NO"
   Implement by _____

   Completion Date: _____.

Self-Care:

Take better care of myself daily by following a healthy routine of self-care each morning, afternoon, and evening.

Start Date: _____

1. Sleep early set a time for sleep at:_____
2. Attend gym, Zumba, personal training, and foundation training by:_____
3. Go for a massage, nails and every three months do my hair.
4. Use natural laundry and bath soap (this is just an example).
5. Take time each day to meditate and reflect on the day.

Completion Date: _____.

Personal Weight management:

Practice healthy eating on a daily basis by eating breakfast, lunch, and dinner at appropriate times.

Set times for _____

1. Follow a healthy diet by decreasing unhealthy foods and write down the foods you will give up and post a list in your refrigerator.

2. Increasing healthy foods: write down healthy foods you will add to your diet and keep on the refrigerator door.
3. Protein shakes before exercise.
4. Add more vegetables to your diet and try new recipes.
5. Drink more water and keep a log.
6. No alcoholic or colored drinks; write down a list.
7. Eat less and do not eat past 7:00 p.m.
8. Avoid heavy metals: do not buy or use cleaning products with toxic chemicals substituted with natural ingredients or organic products like homemade cleaning solutions of vinegar/baking soda.
9. Adapt to natural foods and ingredients.

Completion Date: _____.

Goal 4: Financial freedom- "I want to save 20,000 for a down payment for a house, $5,000 for a vacation and pay off $3,000 in debt."

I would like to save money towards the purchase of a home, save money for a two-week vacation and pay all my debts.

Be committed to spend less weekly, save more monthly

Start date:_____

1. Manage a monthly budget and expenses.
2. Buy items of sale.
3. Use coupons.
4. Keep a locked box with three envelopes for each goal and make weekly or bi-weekly deposits in them towards the goals (each month deposits into savings accounts).
5. Use cloth shopping bags to avoid paying for bags.
6. Cook at home instead of going to restaurants.
7. Make coffee at home instead of buying coffee each day.

8. Follow a budget for food shopping.
9. Manage trips to save on gas.

Completion Date: _____.

Prepare my finances, credit, and expenditures for mortgage approval or business expenses

I would like to work on fixing my credit to be able to qualify for a low interest rate mortgage. I want to manage my credit history by reviewing my credit report/dispute items every six months.

Pay off credit cards by the end of _____.

1. Review credit reports every six months for any errors and dispute unknown charges.
2. Pay off any collection items by:_____.
3. Pay off any medical bills by: _____.
4. Pay off lowest credit and then move towards the next one until you reach the highest paying one and concentrate on this until paid off by: _____.
5. Maintain one major credit card open with low charges by: _____.

Completion Date: _____.

Find a new apartment/buy a house in two years

1. Prepare a list of your dream apartment or home by: _____
2. Write a list of the things that you are looking for that will be a deal maker for you and deal breakers.
3. Learn about house search, investment properties, and what to look for in a good purchase of a home.
4. Look into reliable realtors and start looking for an ideal home.
5. Attend open houses and learn to ask questions about making a good purchase and price negotiation.

6. Save for a down payment by setting aside $100.00 to $200.00 weekly or more if budget allows.

Completion Date: _____.

Goal 5: Personal: "I would like to date to marry. I would like to get married by _____."

I would like to date only marriage-minded men whose words match their actions, present good communication, and are trustworthy.

1. Sign up for a Christian dating app or local single network by: _____.

2. Start dating on marriage minded individuals by: _____.

3. Create a positive profile with positive content and updated photos by: _____.

4. Create a list of what you need or want in a man with red flags to watch for by: _____.

5. Be open to having conversation about marriage by creating a list of questions to ask to determine if you are a good fit by: _____.

6. Set and maintain healthy boundaries while dating.

7. Communicate openly and respectfully.

8. Express feelings, wants, needs and what I do not tolerate.

9. Love more openly, help more often, give more without allowing others to take advantage.

10. Buy a wedding dress.

11. Look into venues.

12. Set a date for marriage to manifest the marriage.

Completion Date: _____.

In this chapter, you have been provided with extensive examples as well as descriptions of several different goals written in detail to provide you with better understanding on goal setting and an illustration of how much you can expand them by clearly stating each task. You can create as many goals as you want to write down as long as they are realistic and are attached to a specific target date. If any of your goals are not fulfilled within the target date, you can carry it over with any goals that were not accomplished to the following six months or the next year. It is recommended that you revise them by describing assigned tasks more in detail and with a realistic target date. Before carrying over the goal to the next six months or the next year, it is advisable to evaluate what stopped you from achieving the goal and explore what you can do better the next time to ensure that you can achieve it. You should determine if the goal is a realistic, purposeful goal for you at this time. Write down what barriers you encounter and why. You want to prevent any barriers or stagnation in achieving your goals, therefore, you want to be clear on why it was not successfully achieved. The following page will introduce you to another more detailed format of goal setting. This is to help you obtain more clarity on goal setting and allow you the freedom to use whatever format works best for you.

Another Example of an Action Plan

This action plan version is a more simplified version of two different frameworks in combination. For those who are familiar with the SWOT analysis, which is more of a strategic management of strengths and weaknesses. This format allows you to document your strengths and weaknesses, target dates, actions steps, and expected outcomes. The other version is the SMART goal framework of goal setting, which is based on measurement of attainable goals by using specific, measurable, achievable, realistic, and time-bound goals, which this format also uses by documenting specific goals, target dates, action steps, accountability, and expected outcomes. If you are an individual who gears toward this format style because you are familiar with this format, it will be an easy form to complete. Also, this action plan is in the form of a table, so many systematic or financially focused individuals may appreciate it. I recommend this format because I have used a similar format when creating goals with staff when I first began in the leadership supervisory role. This format is also for people who like a structured table and seek a more organized way of tracking your goals.

Goals	Strengths	Weakness	Target date	Completion date/ outcome
1. Personal Growth: Personal growth and development can consist of improving education, training, adventure, new experiences, joy, and personal happiness. Write down a goal. Ex: "I would like to obtain training in motivational interviewing and engagement."				

Action steps 1. Sign up for course 2. Practice motivational Interviewing skills **Tools/things needed.** 1. Create an Interviewing skills questions form **Progress** 1. Monitor progress by successful percentage of client engagements				
2. Relationship: Connection with self, family friends, colleagues, and God or church community. Write down a goal. Ex: "I want to connect with a Church community group that focuses on rebuilding relationships." **Action steps** 1. Attend weekly support group for rebuilding relationships **Tools/things needed.** 1. Buy book 10 steps to rebuilding relationships **Progress** 1. Create one or two new friendships 2. Reconnect with family members to mend relationship 3. Practice forgiveness of yourself and others				
3. Health: Improve physical health, including exercise and nutrition, emotional, and mind health including self-care.				

Write down a goal. Ex: "I would like to lose 10 lbs. by the end of next month."				
Action steps 1. Stop eating unhealthy foods 2. Add healthy foods to diet 3. Reduce sugars, fats, and fried foods 4. Drink water instead of juice or soda. **Tools/things needed.** 1. Join a gym 2. *Calorie King* book to check fat, calories, and protein content of foods 3. A scale to weight myself every Monday morning. 4. A journal to document what I eat to identify any unhealthy eating habits. 5. Do not eat in the living room or keep snacks in the living room. **Progress** 1. Write weekly weight loss 2. Keeping tabs on how my clothes fit and document how many inches I lose to track my progress. Document it in a log				
4. Career/Business: Including business, professional development, personal satisfaction, creative expression, and earning a good income. Write down a goal. Ex: "I would like to increase sales by 25% by engaging 10 new clients in the greater metro area of _____." **Action steps** 1. Attend a networking event				

2. Marketing business through social media 3. Run a Groupon campaign offer discount for your first session 4. Join a business networking community. 5. join a FaceBook group **Tools/things needed** 1. Develop an elevator speech to engage people in the community 2. Rebrand or use a marketing campaign 3. Create a blog 4. Offer 30 minutes free introductory sessions **Progress** 1. Identify your target audience 2. Keep tabs on the conversations that landed clients what worked and what did not 3. If you landed the clients write down what was successful 4. If you did not land 10 but landed five, evaluate what worked				
5. Money/Finances: Financial health includes making money, savings, investing, spending on material items, recreation, and travel. Write down goals. Ex: "I would like to save 20% or invest 20% of my sales by _____" or "I would like to learn better financial management by keeping a monthly budget." I will evaluate this budget by: _____ **Action steps** 1. Create a monthly budget to follow				

2. Keep tabs on expenses 3. Buy things on sale 4. Find bargains on things needed. 5. Declutter and sale items not being used 6. Use coupons 7. Take $50.00 each pay period and deposit into savings **Tools/things needed** 1. Monthly budget apps 2. Budget guide book 3. Calculator 4. Coupon organizer/Apps 5. Open a bank account for savings **Progress** 1. Evaluate how the changes have been helping you decrease spending 2. Monitor savings account 3. Noticeable decrease in spending			
6. Giving back or life purpose: What you are meant to be doing, your higher purpose in life, or giving contributions of your time and money to the causes you care about. Write down goal: Ex: "I would like to volunteer for two hrs. a month to a non-profit agency of my choice." "I would like to increase my monthly donation from $50.00 to $100.00 monthly to a non-profit agency or cause starting on: _____." **Action steps** 1. Find an agency to donate for a cause you fill passionate about 2. Do monthly donations of $50.00 3. Volunteer two hrs. a month at different agencies that connect with you			

Tools/things needed 1. Research agencies that you feel connected to 2. Keep track of donations and keep informed of the agency's yearly distribution of donations **Progress** 1. Keep informed how many lives you have changed through your contribution 2. How many hrs. per year you volunteered				

This next chapter is about developing a theoretical framework for your coaching model that will help guide you in servicing your clients. I have included the one I have created and followed as a coaching framework.

Transformational Coaching Model

Mostly all coaches follow a set of theoretical models in which they base their coaching services on. Theoretical frameworks allow you to develop an approach to how you handle clients within their social context, work family, social network, and any past history of trauma or relationship issues. A transformational coaching model lets you evaluate all of these areas in a nonjudgemental way by taking into consideration all these corresponding areas that have influenced the client's life. Let's say a mindset change coach will follow their theoretical model which is "changing mindset" or "mindshift." A confidence coach may focus on "teaching ways to help the client change their own behavior and mindset." A trauma coach may benefit from this model because it allows total transformation in many different areas of the person's life. Another example is that a Christian life coach has a set of principles and theoretical model based on Biblical principles; therefore, their theoretical model is Christian Biblical Principles and applies to daily life along with changing behaviors, mindset, gaining confidence and other areas as well. A personal growth coach focuses on achieving personal growth in the area designated by the client; let's say relationship, spirituality, or career. It is the coach's own choice influenced by the school of thoughts that they identify closely with that will help them gear towards their own theoretical model.

Coaching Perspective- A coach uses a holistic system of identification and a transformational model of change. The coach is an expert who works with raising the client's self-awareness all while empowering, uplifting, and enlightening the client. The coach holds the client accountable in their part of the transformational process as well as identifying their role in their story. Through challenging the client and helping them recognize what is holding them back, the coach will work on establishing solutions and strategies through encouragement, support, and promoting self-changing behaviors also changing to a more positive mindset. The coach will embrace the client's learning style by honoring the client's upbringing environment and how it has influenced the client's mindset. Transformational coaching will focus on self-empowerment of the individual by identifying the client's beliefs that have created fears, barriers, and deterrents in their lives that have stopped them in creating the life they want to live.

Self-Awareness- A life coach has to be able to explore and guide the client to see the big picture of the whole story, using probing questions can engage the client to open up and discuss what they truly feel, what they want, or need in their lives. They do this by using tools that promote further exploration and incite critical thinking, consciously examining how aware the client is of certain behaviors, self-prophecy, fears, self-defeat, and learned behaviors that have been taught in their life journey that has affected their choices by triggering self-sabotage or fear of success.

Perspectives & Attitudes Equal Behaviors- A life coach must be sensitive to the needs, values, and beliefs of the client in order to assist the individual in moving forward in their life journey. Understanding where they are coming from in terms of religion, upbringing, life experiences, and past failures, the life coach can reverently reflect on the client's needs, values, and beliefs system. The life coach can use these as a tool in which to guide the client and achieve progress through the client's own individual perspective. If the life coach fails to respect these areas of the individual, they will lose the client's trust.

Exploring Options and Taking Action: Empowering Positive Choices- Once the client is able to understand themselves and reach self-awareness, they will be open to taking risks by taking action steps towards their goals. During this phase, they will either experience pre-contemplation or the motivation to change or take action. The life coach will then work with the client in exploring options and guide the client in developing an action plan that is person centered and verbally created by the client. This may be a difficult transition for some clients to be in and they may feel stuck due to past experiences. As a result, it can affect the client by creating barriers that prevent them from taking a proactive action due to past failures, fear, and self-beliefs. The life coach will then counteract this by helping the client identify those negative patterns of thinking and using imagery to focus on future positive outcomes. The life coach will challenge the client to continue to explore their core beliefs and their own self-defeating persona by supporting the client to release whatever is acting as a deterrent in their life and release it from the inside out in order to effectively move forward.

Empowering Questions: Tools to Equip You For Life- The next step for the life coach is to ask empowering questions that can incite the client to think proactively. By asking empowering questions, it will be a catalyst for the client to reach their own findings or solutions. For example, questions like: "What do you think is a solution to this dilemma that keeps you stagnant in your career?" and "What do you need that will help you to take the first step towards a change in career?"

throw the ball back into the client's hands while the life coach waits to receive back the client's conscious solution to their own difficulty. The focus is placed on the individual client in order to assist him/her to recognize and to reach a sense of empowerment that will allow them to move forward and take positive action.

Personal Growth: Growing Both Inside and Outside- The ultimate challenge for the client is to reach the self fulfillment of personal growth in all the areas of his/hers life that have been unbalanced or stagnant. The life coach will be mindful of the client's progress and celebrate all success. The focal point of transformational coaching is to instill hope, faith, motivation, and guidance via transformational empowerment to face what most challenges the client with honor, respect, integrity, and accountability with the utmost goal in mind to reach self-empowered living.

Environmental Systems

Individual: Finding the Source or Core- The life coach will help guide the client in exploring and identifying their present environment ("Who and where am I?"). The life coach will challenge the client to see if they are just doing or being or just going with the flow of life without experiencing the joy of being in a place in which they can be truly happy. Through guided imagery, the client will take a journey into self-exploration to visualize where they want to be and what they need, and what they want to truly achieve.

Behaviors: Evaluate the Story to Identify Self-defeating Behaviors- The life coach will help the client explore their personal stories and identify behaviors that have caused negative choices and consequences. Through creating new stories and asking "What will I do differently?" or "How can I change my story?" The coach will guide the client in examining any patterns of negative thinking that have influenced behaviors that have affected their life choices and also stunt personal growth.

Capabilities: Seeking to Know and Find Hidden Talents and Gifts- The life coach will guide the client in seeking from within his or hers inner gifts, talents, and creativity, using these capabilities to create a life where they can use their gifts, talents, and creativity wholeheartedly and also learn how to enhance them further. "What do I need to learn and how?" The life coach will assist the client with evaluating options that will assist them in finding his/her answers on how and what skills they need to learn that can bring them to their next level.

Values and Beliefs: Identifying Values and Beliefs and How They Can be Used for Progress- The life coach will use effective tools to assist the client in identifying their values and beliefs that have affected their progress. The coach will guide the client to increase new values and beliefs that can help develop personal growth by creating a new mindset. "What is important?" and "What no longer works in my life?" or "What is needed in this new journey of growth?"

Identity: Finding Who You Are- The life coach will challenge the client with coaching tools to help explore ways that can help him/her find out who they truly are at the core and bring forth a new persona who values and accepts who they are at the core and what she/he offers the world. "Who am I really?" Who you were and what you will become is a total transformation into a new beginning.

Vision: Purpose and Vision- The life coach will create a safe and neutral environment for which the client can express without reservations their true-life purpose and vision. The life coach will use tools that can help the client sort out values, mission in life, and appraise their spirituality and connectedness to a high power. As a result, the client will find balance, and this will help them feel connected to a higher source. "What am I part of?" Reaching high and seeking a higher plane where it is easy to connect to the source and find your divine purpose.

Outcome: The client is the director of his/her own story and must figure out where they are heading in their life journey through trial and error. The coach is the facilitator that ensures that the set is ready and decorated with different choices of scenery. The life coach must allow the client the freedom to reflect on past choices or events that have affected their ability to move forward in their journey. When the client reaches a peak point in their own self-awareness; they will be able to evaluate what they are doing right, where they have been successful, and what needs to be fixed as well as what they can change to become more productive in their own lives.

Transformational Coaching Model Outcome

1. The Individual:

Becoming resilient, committed to change, self-determined, self-empowered, knowing who they are and what they are capable of, and what they contribute to society. Knowing how to balance their life, practicing self-care, knowing his/hers limitations, and exercising appropriate boundaries.

2. Evaluating Relationships:

Using what they have learned to enhance personal relationships - family, partner, husband, health services, church, employment, and peers.

3. Acceptance:

Learning how to accept attitude, personality, weaknesses, strengths, ideologies of culture, others perspective, and conducting self-introspection when necessary.

4. Changes:

Learning how to effectively relate, react, respond and deal with challenges, crisis, partner, husband, friends, family, neighbors, and legal or social systems.

5. Changes & Outcomes:

What will be achieved is an overall personal transformation and growth in all areas of life.

The next chapter is about embracing change and how ready you are to change. Do you know what change brings? Next chapter will help you explore what you need to make changes in your life.

Embracing Change

Why is it important to embrace change? Change is good and it promotes growth in all areas of our lives. But we must want it, be open to it, and embrace it. It is not for the faint of heart as you will undergo a process like that of a butterfly metamorphosis. It is required in order for you to become the person you desire to be. "Don't rush. Don't lose focus, Believe in your vision and your action plan. Wait for some time before you think of making any change in your idea." —Pooja Agnihotri.

It is important to allow change to happen gradually without rushing it or moving too quickly. It's like the example of growing a plant. If you try to alter the process, there is no guarantee that it will produce more or healthier fruits. It is best to allow the process to happen without altering its change. Just trust the process. Change is necessary in many aspects of the word. First and foremost, we must change certain behaviors in our character that affect our progress or where God is leading us to, letting go of certain habits, places, and things that are obstacles rather than helping to push you forward towards your dreams. Change is a chance to begin anew with a more focused and objective mindset. Change is a metamorphosis process of growth. It starts with a slow process of development, isolation, and self-introspection. The process of change is one of uprooting. You can feel a certain atmospheric feeling of which time shows an outgrowing of where you are, what you do and how you view yourself in your life. It is a euphoric feeling that something is going to be taking place in your life because you are starting to anticipate it and know that you are changing. The process of shedding layers of the old has started. To better explain this process in a more vivid and creative way, I am going to share a short blog that I wrote in April 2022, and it is titled "Metamorphosis of a Butterfly."

On April 17, 2022, I was listening to the Christian radio station, and they were talking about the fact that there are 17,000 species of butterflies. This made me extremely happy since I love butterflies. In my creative mind, I visualized that when God was creating the butterflies, He saw how beautiful they looked, and He might have said, "I want one in this color, and another one in that color, in this size, and how about this unique imprint? I love them all!" The Lord in His creativity took His time in perfection of the butterfly. Don't quote me on this as this is just how my mind thinks! You can see that He created them uniquely, intrinsically beautiful! "Intrinsic means belonging to the essential nature or constitution of a thing." The intrinsic worth of a butterfly. It's set apart from all others! Perfectly woven in majesty by the hands of God. If ever you doubted God's existence, stop for a minute and take a look at the butterflies. See how intrinsic, unique, and purposeful the process is of becoming one. The Lord knew that, in creating this beautiful masterpiece, it would come with a beautiful story of change and of how it came about! A hard process of change, pain, and pushing forward to become that beautiful butterfly that finally gets to spread its wings!

I can tell you this - in everything that God does, there is purpose, and it's beautiful. In the same manner, it relays to us all! Psalm 139:13-14, "For you created my inmost being; you knit me together in my mother's womb. I am fearfully, and wonderfully made." I am going to stop right there because this Psalm has such an in-depth meaning about how God knows us, creates us, and knows everything about us! You see, just like the butterfly, He has given each one of us a beautiful purpose that we sometimes don't even have a clue about. However, we know deep down that it will help others heal, be encouraged, or become closer to God. You see, butterflies are special and so are you! Embrace the power of change and become the beautiful being God purposefully made you to be! This story is to encourage all readers that while the process of change is one of difficulties, the final product is one of ease and beauty. Next are thought-provoking questions to help you familiarize yourself with the process of change.

Questions

Embracing Change

15. Change is not easy. It's difficult; it demands commitment and dedication to embrace the process. What changes do you need in your life, character, career, relationships, etc. that will help you become a better prepared person? Are you willing to put in the work required? Do you understand that the process of change is painful and demands excruciating detachment from people, places, and things? How does that make you feel and knowing this you are still open to change? And once you get there, what do you intend to do to help you stay grounded in this process of change? What do you hope to achieve in changing these character traits, career, relationships, or way of life?

_____

_____

_____

_____

_____

_____

_____

_____

_____

_____

_____

_____

Change Process

"See I am doing a new thing! Now it springs up; do you not perceive it? I am making a way in the wilderness and streams in the wasteland." —Isaiah 43:19

As you get closer to your breakthrough and closer to becoming visible in your new purpose, you will find yourself overwhelmed going through many challenges, which you feel like almost throwing in the towel and giving up. What will you do when this happens? Do you feel strong enough to overcome the challenge and difficulties? Are you willing to embrace the change process? Let's take those small steps towards our process.

There is an amazing, thought-provoking quote by Leo Tolstoy that states, "Everyone thinks of changing the world, but no one thinks of changing himself." This is a deep quote because it reflects that change must start deep within us. We are responsible for changing ourselves first in order to create change or be a catalyst of change for the world. This change in us catapults us into reflecting on our inner core and in looking at everything that we have been holding onto that will not be productive in this new journey that we are walking into. Therefore, this change that we must make requires letting go of old habits, attitudes, and any other personality hindrance that may sabotage our change process. How does change happen? Change sometimes happens impromptu or precipitated by outside forces and situations that force us to change. How we adjust to it determines how we will thrive in different situations. We must not allow the difficult experiences to ruffle us or cause us to become bent out of shape or lose our joy. It is ok to have bad days as this is part of life! But don't allow those bad days to continue robbing you of your peace when you do not witness progress or see the change reflecting an outcome that you are hoping for. After all, we are only human, and sometimes, we let our emotions become weak. We become vulnerable by reacting to negative situations that are just bumps on the road but are manageable for us to go over them with ease when we see them for what they are. This is where self-care comes into place. Taking the time to process negative situations by not reacting but responding in a manner that will keep you safe emotionally as you address the circumstances appropriately. Sometimes it will require taking a step back to regroup and start over. There is a quote by Melody Beattie that goes like this, "Letting go helps us to live in a more peaceful state of mind and helps restore our balance. It allows others to be responsible for themselves and for us to take our hands off situations that do not belong to us. This frees us of unnecessary stress." This does not mean that you are weak or have given up. No, not all, this means that you have made a decision to place yourself first to take care of yourself so that you can become stronger and better empowered to continue the journey. It's about finding the balance again, regroup, and make necessary changes within yourself in order to grow. It may even result in taking a break for a few weeks to help you gain a clean and fresh perspective on the changes that you need to make.

In order to see growth within the change process, one must be willing and open to make adjustments in their life when they see these types of things happen. I like using analogies to bring forth visual clarity and understanding. This is from a blog I wrote a few years back reflecting the process of change.

Water is a constant, radical process of change that we hardly pay attention to. And if we pay close attention to it, we can find valuable insights. Therefore, we must be like water! Why be like water? Water flows sometimes without direction; it is pure, clear, and adjusted to practically any shape and size. Water is the most needed liquid and sustains life with its many uses which benefit us. For example, we drink it, use it for cooking, to feed plants, to bathe, and use it to wash dirt away. Water is refreshing, renewable, and conducts electricity! We can find many important multiple functions of water. In Genesis 1:2, "And the earth was without form, and void; and darkness was upon the face of the deep. And the Spirit of God moved upon the face of the waters." In the beginning of creation, God's spirit moved within the water. The word "move" is referenced to mean action or movement forward, which can demonstrate a process of change requiring movement or action.

For example, water can transmit movements in the form of waves that can produce a process of change through the adding of sound, frequencies, radio, or sonar waves. According to the research of a Japanese scientist Dr. Masaru Emoto, "Water is the mirror that has the ability to show us what we cannot see." Doctor Emoto goes on to share that if you speak words to the water and crystallize it, it will demonstrate a reaction of positive or negative depending on the word's use! We also can become reactant to situations that make us feel positive or negative too! And in the words of Bruce Lee, "Be like water making its way through cracks. Do not be assertive, but adjust to the object, and you shall find a way around or through it. If nothing within you stays rigid, outward things will disclose themselves. Empty your mind to be formless. Shapeless like water. If you put water into a cup, it becomes a cup. You put water into a bottle, and it becomes the bottle. You put it in a teapot; it becomes the teapot. Now water can flow, or it can crash. Be water my friend."

This, my friends, is the most amazing description of how to adjust to changes, challenges, or difficult situations that can affect our flow, growth, and where we need to be! Like water which accommodates to the environmental changes it experiences, we are to learn how to make those adjustments to accommodate the new flow of where we should be moving towards without becoming stagnant. Change requires adaptability - the more that you embrace change, the more adaptable you are to situations, things, or life happenings that often disrupt the flow of the water of life and where it is taking us.

Then what must we do is be like water and allow ourselves to flow in a new direction. This direction may be better and smoother and bring you a clearer vision on where it is leading you too. Lastly, changes must happen in order for us to grow. Colossians 3:10, "And have put the new self, which is being renewed in knowledge after the image of its creator." Psalms 18:2, "Create in me a clean heart, O God, and renew a right spirit within me." We let go of the old, of what used to be, what we lost, and what we gave up. In order for God to bless you with the new blessings, he is asking for a blank state, to be like water so that all can see the difference. Your life will be living proof that it was God all along who has been blessing you! Be like water - easily adaptable to allow the blessings to flow! Don't be afraid of change, even if change makes you feel uncomfortable or experience fear. It is the fear of the unknown, of "What if?" What if something goes wrong or what if I am not good enough. And many other "what ifs." This is normal and you must evaluate where this fear is stemming from, and confront it head on. But "what if" everything goes better than what you expected? What if it instills new growth and progress in your life and in your business? Change is good! Change is growth, change is healthy, and change will bring you many added blessings. Feel the fear and allow it to push you towards the end goal.

The following section will provide you with some questions that will push you to think of yourself and areas that you need to change. This will help you to start thinking about change at a different angle of "How can it benefit me, what will it bring me, and what do I expect of this change?"

Questions

Change Process

16. What are some things in your personality that you feel that you need to change? Do you feel like it will be hard to change those thoughts, behaviors, and ways of being? How will it help you in your business? What do you understand by the word "adaptability?" Are you able to adapt to different situations? The term "be like water," what does it mean to you? Are you open to learning new ways of doing things and changing some old ways of doing things?

_____

_____

_____

_____

_____

_____

_____

_____

_____

_____

_____

_____

_____

Adjusting to a New Life

Why adjust? The Cambridge dictionary defines adjusting as, "To change something slightly, especially to make it more correct, effective, or suitable." This involves making subtle changes first and then major changes that require an adjustment period. You will need to become disciplined and balanced in your life. This will help you adjust to everything that this change will require of you to let go and adapt to a new way of being. What can you let go of things that no longer serve you to help you adjust to a new life?

I mentioned in the prior chapter that changes bring an adjustment period in which you may feel uncomfortable, experience pain, and feelings of uncertainty. This is normal to feel, and it is important to learn how to embrace it because, if you fight the adjustments, you will struggle spiritually, physically, and mentally. The process of adaptation is also uncomfortable but is most needed. "Adaptation is a profound process. It means you figured out how to thrive in the world." Learning how to adapt to shifts in our lives requires a period of preparation. You must prepare yourself for this phase by taking better care of your physical, mental, and spiritual life through prayer and fasting. This is also the time of preparation in which you realize that instead of worrying about all the hardships that you are experiencing, you should focus on expressing gratitude, demonstrating gratitude in everything and anything you do. We all have to make adjustments in our lives throughout our journey, and when we enter a different shift or phase in our journey, it's nerve wracking because it comes unexpectedly. It comes without a warning but waves a flag imprinted with the words, "YOU MUST ADJUST." It may sound forceful, but it slowly warns you to be prepared, be ready, and understand that this too must happen. It's really not that difficult to make adjustments but we make it hard on ourselves because some things in our lives have become so habitual that they are hard to break free from.

When we know, we must let go! For example, healthy eating is one area in our lives that we all struggle with, and it is a great example to use. Let's say that your doctor has advised you that your eating habits are affecting your health. What do you do? How do you react? Are you accepting the reality that your health is in danger? When we first hear it, we become afraid or resistant to change. And in order to change this unwarranted diagnosis of your health being at risk, we must take small steps to change our eating habits and so we start to slowly adapt to our new way of eating healthier. And with this new adaptation, it will also change our mindset about eating once we become disciplined within the process of adapting to healthy eating. However, there will be planned cheat days and there will be other times where it is unplanned because you cannot say no to someone offering you unhealthy food, or perhaps a dessert that you so much love is offered. But what works for this process is being consistent and acknowledging when you have failed to follow the healthy eating and then moving on by getting back on track, thus adapting back to the change. And like everything, the more you do it, the stronger and the healthier you become. It is not until we see those results of our consistency that we become more open and motivated to continue to adjust our eating habits and become better balanced in our eating.

I learned this from my fitness coach; I have an excellent fitness coach who I worked with for a year when I was struggling with some medical issues, and he kept me on track. Although he is my son, he was harder on me than all of his clients. I appreciate his approach because it kept me focused and on track with my fitness journey. I have been able to witness excellent results. I had to learn how to adapt to making these tough decisions and adapt to a new way of healthy eating and self-care. In the same way, adaptation requires that responsibility of staying disciplined and knowing that adapting to change will benefit us in the long run.

Whether in your career, family, relationships, or self-care, learning to easily adapt to change is a strength that makes you more competitive in the workforce, in life, and in relationships. The more you learn to adapt and embrace the process of change that it brings, the more tools in your toolbox that you will have. It creates more opportunities, more choices, and personal growth. In the next page, you will be able to answer some questions that can help you identify what areas you have been able to adapt to and recognize if it was difficult or an easy process for you.

Questions

Adjusting to a New Life

17. We must work on ourselves by obtaining inner healing from some wounds that may still be lingering and affecting our emotions and wellbeing. To do this, we must learn how to effectively adapt to new situations, places, and processes of change that produce discomfort. What are some things in your inner self that you have been holding onto that have prevented you from becoming your true best self? What are some things that you must adjust to in order to become successful in your new journey? Do you remember a time or place in which you had to adapt to changes, whether in your career or personal life? How did you manage those changes and how did it make you feel? Were they easy or hard to adapt to?

_____

_____

_____

_____

_____

_____

_____

_____

_____

_____

Staying Committed

Commitment means staying dedicated to your goals and it requires responsibility to stay on course. What does it take for you to stay committed to your dream? This one is a serious question because if we are not committed, we will not be able to stay focused on the ultimate outcome or fulfill our process towards our objective. Staying committed also requires consistency and being able to do what you need to in order to move forward, even when lacking resources, connections, or the support. In the words of Jim Rohn, "Motivation is what gets you started. Commitment is what keeps you going." Being committed is the desire to make it, and once you lack commitment, you are bound to fail.

Now, the challenge is to stay committed to the mission, vision, and goal plan of following your purpose and destiny for your life. Staying focused is a priority and adapting to changes! But most important is becoming committed to making it come to live. Your dreams are yours, and only you have the responsibility to work on them and in staying consistent until it is manifested in your life. Believe me, everything and anything will happen to divert your focus and make you want to give up. It is a time of challenges, trials, and tribulations that will make you feel frustrated or unmotivated at times. Staying motivated is part of the process of staying committed. Being motivated to also stay consistent in keeping your word, that no matter what you do, you will keep working on your goals come hell or high waters. This means "come what may." You will be determined to persevere. You will need to be open to embracing and adapting to the changes that will eventually come with these new responsibilities. Motivation is that reagent that will help you to adjust to the changes that you must make at a personal and professional level in yourself. Being committed to staying motivated will also help you celebrate and embrace the new you and your new life as a changed woman or man. This acceptance of staying motivated will set a pattern of success for others to follow. Another personal commitment is one that requires a solid agreement within yourself to stay focused on the end goal. Commitment then demands for you to follow through with action-oriented behaviors. Let's say you are committed to coaching five people for free for 30 minutes as a way to pay it forward. You must follow through by advertising it, seeking out the clients, and following through your commitment to coaching those five people. It's about following through and being consistent. Commitment also requires you to set the time you need to work on your goals or business in order to make it happen. It means managing time accordingly, rejecting distractions, and being consistent to take responsibility to keep pushing towards your goals. The next page includes questions that will assist you in learning how committed you are or have been in prior situations that will help you gain clarity on how important it is to stay committed to your goals.

Questions

Staying committed

18. Staying committed will demand that whenever you feel rejected, or you want to give up, you pick yourself up and stay true to yourself by continuing to pursue your dreams. What are some strengths that you possess that will help you stay committed? Do you have any difficulties in keeping and staying focused? Do you easily become offended when someone speaks negatively about you? If so, how do you handle it? Can you think of new ways to handle negative comments? How committed and dedicated do you feel you are?

_____

_____

_____

_____

_____

_____

_____

_____

_____

_____

_____

_____

Reaching New Heights in Life

Growth comes with new heights, new responsibilities, and new ways of doing things. Are you ready to take on the challenge of new responsibilities? Even after following a routine for so many years, the new heights will keep you on your toes with different activities. Think of ways that you can maintain yourself organized throughout a hectic week of activities and busyness of life. "Being an entrepreneur isn't just a job title, and it isn't just about starting a company. It's a state of mind. It's about seeing connections others can't, seizing opportunities others won't, and forging new directions that others haven't."

When you are finally reaching your goals, and they are coming into reality, there will be many doors that will become open for you to step through and reach new heights in your life. However, all doors may not benefit you, so you have to choose carefully. And with new heights, there will come greater responsibility, which means that you have to act as that role model that God has anointed you to be. Also, God will be using your life and testimony to help others grow in their own life. Reaching new heights means that you will be able to give back to others who need a word of encouragement, a listening ear, and/or financial support. God will bless you with enough so that you can bless others with the gifts He has given you. How ready are you to start this challenge? How do you feel about having to fill this role in your life? Do you feel confident in being in high demand? How do you currently manage your schedule?

Once your business is up and running, you will be expected to be part of the community or attend events as a guest speaker. You will be seen as a role model for other coaches as well as mentor those who will need your guidance. This will translate into high demand and becoming busy with clients, events, marketing, and managing social media, so your business can continue to thrive.

It will require from you a high level of commitment in order to stay focused and organized. To stay organized, you will need many different tools to stay on top of appointments, clients, events, and other activities unless you hire an assistant or marketing person to assist you with all tasks. For example, making sure that you manage your online calendar of appointments on your website. Perhaps keeping a white board to write down daily tasks, follow up or outreach, timing yourself between appointments, or using an appointment and task managers like Toggl. This will help you stay organized and on task will help you be productive as well as providing quality services, even while having a high quantity of clients. You will know what will work best for you and that will help you stay focused and on track with your business. The importance of being present, consistent, and on top of things demands a level of balancing in-house tasks, outside tasks, and all business functions like scheduling and accounting on top of creating new content, blogs, and all social media apps to keep your business afloat and competitive in the market. The following questions will help explore your level of preparedness to soar at a level of high demands that will help you see what areas you will need to work on and what areas you have already mastered.

Questions

Reaching New Heights in Life

19. When you hear the words "Reaching New Heights in Life," what do they mean to you? How do they make you feel? What do they entail for you? What doors do you feel you need to open? Think of your story and how it can impact others to reach new heights - how would you relate what you had to overcome in your life? How can you use those skills to help others? Think of ways you can start to become better organized. What will be the first step you will take to stay on track? How do you handle success? Will you stay grounded and humble? If so, how will that look to you?

_____

_____

_____

_____

_____

_____

_____

_____

_____

_____

_____

Blessings

"And from his fullness we have received, grace upon grace," John 1:16. "And God is able to make grace abound to you, so that all sufficiently in all things at all times, you may abound in every good work," 2nd Corinthians 9:8. "And God is able to make all grace abound toward you so that you, always having all sufficiency in all things, may have an abundance for every good work." This Bible verse shows us that if we place our trust in God, He will bless us with everything we need. Because all blessings come with the obedience to His guidance, confirmation, and in allowing Him to be first in our lives. If we step out in faith, we will experience His abundance. "Free yourself from the complexities and drama of your life. Simplify. Look within. Within ourselves we all have the gifts and talents we need to fulfill the purpose with which we've been blessed."
—Steve Maroboli

The blessings of God are sacred. Why do I say sacred? I say sacred because God's blessings are permanent and without conditions. The word sacred found in the Vine's Expository Dictionary page 984, is the Greek word "HIEROS," which means "consecrated to God." Why must you keep it sacred? The reason is that the minute you divert from this sacredness, you allow the darkness to come in and distort what God has given us. In another note, there is a common practice amongst the Jewish culture, in which they follow a set of ethics and principles. More so when starting their own businesses, operating their daily business practices, conducting business with other people, or supporting others with theirs. The Jewish culture also has other generational traditions about helping their own family members with start-up businesses. In fact, the Jewish culture follows strict guidelines when conducting or starting a business based on several sacred ancient principles that they follow in order to guarantee success and blessings.

One of the principles that I want to highlight is one that they apply not only in business but in all of their relationships. The top principle is to not desecrate the name of God, which translates that in all business practices one must be loyal and honest in the sight of God. Therefore, a person will not conduct business with another person if the person does not follow these ethical principles. Another interesting fact about Jewish culture is that they wake up first thing each morning in gratitude and pray to God for their lives, for being restored to another day, and express thankfulness for their blessings including their business. This tradition is based on Psalm 111, "Fear of God is the beginning of wisdom." I saw a video of a person on social media explaining the value of saying this morning prayers, and she emphasized that they witness an overflowing of blessings in all areas of their lives because the first thing that they do is give God thanks for their blessings. I think that this is a great tradition to follow because God should be first in everything we do. Another reason is that expressing gratitude each day allows you to first feel blessed each morning because you connected yourself with the creator and expressed gratitude to Him. It also attracts blessings because you are expressing gratitude, and this opens doors of blessings.

Therefore, blessings may come in many forms, but remember that these blessings are what God has confirmed will benefit you and keep you grounded. He is also aware of any others that will only bring you destruction or make you turn away from him. Believe that He will give you warnings about these blessings that are not beneficial to you, and He will leave it up to you to be obedient. Although, prior to receiving the blessings you will experience testing, trials, and challenges. These are necessary in order for you to gain maturity, learn, and experience personal growth that will allow you handle the blessings He is about to give you. God's blessings come with peace and harmony and will help you grow in all areas of your life. The favor of God is abundant enough to open doors no man can close or no obstacle can stand in the way of.

The favor of God will bring the right people with the right mindset and with the right intentions to bless you in what God is working on in your life. The favor of God will bring grace and mercy in all situations that present itself to harm you or stop you, and He will turn it around for your good.

You know when they are blessings and when they are barriers masked as blessings because sometimes the enemy intercepts certain doors to lead you to the wrong path. And since God is watching over you, He will protect you by opening a new door and shifting some things around for your good. With that being said, what will you do when you reach the highest pinnacle of success? How will you proceed? How will you react? What will you do with the instructions He has given you? The following pages will introduce you to a story I wrote back in 2020 titled "The Highest Mountain" as an example of trying to reach your blessings while rushing through shortcuts and detours or by hurrying the process without thinking of the negative consequences attached to each choice. It is for those who compromised their blessings by accepting less than what God has intended for them to have because they felt lonely or tired in the journey, or they gave up the fight to shift forward. To those who altogether waved the white flag of surrender and as a result accepted a menial life less than what God had intended for them because they have allowed the pressures, manipulation, and negative projection of others dictate how they feel, think, and what they should do. That it has affected their ability to see with clarity to where God was leading them too. I have broken down the story in short paragraphs with reflective questions to help you practice the lesson and understand where you are at in your journey.

Questions

Blessings

20. Think of a time in which you felt blessed. How did it make you feel? What did you do with these blessings? Blessings come in many forms and in many ways; think of how you would like to bless others once you have the resources to help. What do you consider a godly blessing in your life? Making a difference in someone else's life - what does that mean to you? Will you be able to discern a door of blessings versus a counterfeit door?

_____

_____

_____

_____

_____

_____

_____

_____

_____

_____

_____

_____

_____

The Highest Mountain

The highest mountain came about after reading the Bible in Mark 9:2: "Now after six days Jesus took Peter, James, and John and led them up to a high mountain apart by themselves: and He was transfigured before them." This Bible verse may not relate to life coaching, but reaching the highest mountain is the achievement of victory and being transfigured is a process of transformation. The mountain mentioned is the highest snowy peak of Mount Hermon, and it is the highest in all of Palestine. I want to start this chapter by asking you "What are you looking for? And do you know where you are going?" Think about these two questions when you read each chapter of the story. I wrote this story back in May 2020 before moving to Florida to remind those who read the story not to forget where they came from once they achieve their goals, and also not to take any shortcuts when trying to reach their dreams. A simple reminder to not let the enemy tempt them into selling themselves out of God's blessing for their lives. Everything takes time, and sometimes getting there progressively is better than rushing into it. The important thing is not to quit before the breakthrough.

"Don't quit. You keep walking. You keep trying. There is help and happiness ahead. Some blessings come soon, some come late, and some don't come until heaven; but for those who embrace the gospel of Jesus Christ, they come. It will be all right in the end. Trust God and believe in good things to come."—Jeffrey R. Holland

This is the story of a young man (can also relate to a young woman as well) who challenged himself to climb the highest mountain. The highest mountain can be compared to the highest pinnacle of success. The young man is extremely ambitious and determined. He felt ready to take on this new challenge in his life; after all, he was young and still learning about life. On the way to the mountain, the road was rocky, the pavement rough, steep, and hot. On the pathway, he encountered boulders and tree branches that blocked the road, making it hard to jump over the obstacles. As a result, most times he had to deviate by walking in the grass, near the trees, until the road to the pathway became visible again to enter and follow. Being young has it's advantage as he was strong and with stamina to sometimes move them to clear the pathway towards his journey.

After walking religiously up and down the road and climbing uphill, he saw in the distance an apparition of what looked like an older man. This man appeared like time had caught up to him; his hair was gray, visibly thinning, and his body also appeared as though the years had taken a toll on his body as he walked on his path, and he had a distinguished limp. He was carrying a small backpack and dressed sporty but conservative with a hat hanging over his neck and sunglasses over his head. The young man walked closer toward the direction of the old wise man. The old man was just sitting on a large rock, taking a break, sipping water from a green, safari-looking water bottle that looked just like him - a little rough and worn out.

The young man curiously stopped and asked, "How did you manage to climb this far?" He was of older age and hardly looked like an able-body to climb such a high peak. Sometimes appearances can be deceiving and like the saying goes "you can't judge a book by its cover" meaning that sometimes we underestimate individuals by how they look or other attributes, that we forget that behind the person is a well rounded seasoned individual with great versatility, knowledge, and excellent resources to offer that can help you grow in your journey.

The old man said, "Young man, good question. I took my time, you see, and then waited until mid-afternoon when the sun was not hitting as hard to walk up to avoid the sun rays, and now I am taking a quick break."

The young man said to the old wise man, "You are wasting your time, taking breaks; soon enough it will get dark." The young man then said, "Do you really think that you can climb up to the top?" The young man did not see the old man as a wise man with experience, no, not at all. But he saw him as someone who was old and washed out, not able to keep up with the pace of going uphill to the highest pinnacle of the mountain because in the eyes of the young man, he did not have what it took to make it. And like the younger generation would say, "Ok Boomer, let's see you do it!" The young man never asked the old man how he was going to do it, or if he had done it before, or how much experience he had climbing, but instead he viewed it as impossible for him to accomplish this feat due to his age. On the next page, you will have an opportunity to explain your take on this short story and elaborate on why and what is the message being conveyed.

Questions

The Highest Mountain

21. What did you understand about this short paragraph, or what do you feel is the moral of this story? What role does the old man have in this journey? Now, let's transpose it into a business journey; what is more important - to get there faster or to learn better skills progressively? Does it matter how fast you reach a pivotal point in your career? Or are there other things of more importance in life? How do you feel if you encounter someone in your journey who may have more resources than you? What would be the benefit to you, if it seems like they are getting better results than you? How will you feel about this and what will be your reaction? How can you turn it around to work for you?

_____

_____

_____

_____

_____

_____

_____

_____

_____

_____

_____

_____

What Happens When You Aim to Get to the Mountain Top Without Placing God First

Striving to get to your pinnacle of success faster and easier does not bring true security or build a strong financial foundation as is needed. I am not sure if you have heard the saying "what goes up, must come down." This may be true for some people who rush in, trying to get to the highest mountain of success but failing to place God first in their lives. When God is first, and we don't lean on our own understanding, things fall in place and the storm or stress of worrying about making money doesn't ruffle your feathers because we are trusting in God and God alone. We find ways to figure out God's provision for our lives. "When we put God first, all other things fall into their proper place or drop out of our lives. Our love of the Lord will govern the claims for our affection, the demands on our time, the interests we pursue, and the order of our priorities."
—Ezra Taft Benson

Continuing on with the story, the old man who, through time, had acquired much wisdom and expertise, not visible in the physical but instilled in the old man's heart and mind, asked the young man the following:

"Young man, what do you think is the most important thing in life?" Sometimes we have to take a moment and reflect on this phrase. Especially, if you are in a hurry to get to where you want to be that you forget what is most important. Those moments that you will never get back, the time you can't go back to, and the opportunities that you had to share with loved ones that you missed. This is not saying that you must not work hard to achieve your goals or dedicate the time to achieve. But it is reminding us of the purpose to create more balance, more time, and more important moments in life. One example I can think of is Steve Jobs who stated, "My favorite things in life don't cost any money. It's really clear that the most precious resource we all have is time."

The clever young man looked at him and said, "To accomplish as much as you can. As time flies, you do whatever it takes to get to the top and say, 'I am on top of the Highest Peak of Mountain.'" The young man quickly ignored the old man and started walking towards the path without elaborating on his answers as he continued walking and hurrying off, as if there was a fire behind him, and he was running away from it. The young man did not even stop to take a break this time as he seemed in such a hurry. The old wise man, deep in thought, continued with patience, ease, and calm. The young man continued to hurry to the next pinnacle of the climb as if the pinnacle was going to be moved somewhere else, and finally, after a few hours, he stopped and took a break to rest. The old man became visible again, walking slowly as he was old and had walked for several hours to reach the same location but within his pace.

When he quickly saw that the young man was appearing tired and worn out, the old man told him, "You probably should rest; would you like some water?"

The young man told him, "No, I am ok, I have everything I need in my backpack." The young man again refused the old man's assistance and again hurried off and started to walk with haste to reach the peak before the end of the day! Sometimes, we aim to get where we want to be in a hurry to get to the place we think we need to be first to achieve our dreams. We forget to rest, reflect, or appreciate the people that extend their support. The next questions will help you reflect on this section and contemplate on the question, "What do you think is the most important thing in life?"

Questions

Like this young man, we often aim to get to the mountain top without placing God first

22. What do you think are the most important things in life? How important is it for you to take time for children, friends, and family? The young man seemed in a hurry; do you think this is productive when establishing a business? If not, why? And how is taking time for yourself important? What do you do that helps you take care of your wellbeing? Are you able to rest?

_____

_____

_____

_____

_____

_____

_____

_____

_____

_____

_____

_____

_____

_____

We Like to Do Things our Own Way, Right?

Sometimes, we think we have all the answers or know the best route to take. We forget to ask God for guidance and allow him to lead us on the path. God should be first in every decision that you make. Ask him in prayers for clarity, guidance, and confirmation as to what road you should take. Bob Proctor states "You do not become a real pro in your field by doing certain things - you become a pro in your field by doing things a certain way." This means that while rushing to make it may appear practical, it may not be the most productive. What is more important is the manner in which we arrive and how we handle the challenges. The journey is an essential lesson for learning new ways of doing things.

The old man stopped and warned the young man, "There are dangerous roads ahead! Always remember to look to your right and to look to your left, but always keep your focus on pushing and moving forward. And as much as you want to look back, do not look back, not even to swipe a mosquito off your back or when you get tempted to measure the distance." (These are representations of the distractions of the present or past and of things that the enemy uses to distract us from our purpose.)

The young man, bold and proud, said to the old wise man, "I know every rule to the climb, and I will be just fine. And if I need to find something, I can just Google it and find the answers right away." The young man stood confident, tall, and proud as if he knew everything there is to know about climbing the highest mountain.

The old wise man said, "Good luck young man, remember, don't look back." The young man soon enough hurried himself back to the tracks in desperation to finish first and finish fast. As he did not see the value of the words that the wise old man had told him.

The young man totally ignored the warning, and so confidently began chanting, "I am strong, I am fast, I am witty, and I am smart," and "I will get there before the old man." The young man, determined to beat the old wise man, felt reassured that he had it all figured out.

The old man told the young man faintly in hopes that he could hear him, "Ok, but just be warned..." He did not allow the old man to finish what he had to say before he disappeared like the nightfall. The old man sat quietly, calmly, and focused and decided to eat his meal and rest. Walking in the dark is dangerous, so he decided to set up camp and wait till early morning break to start his walk again.

He confidently awaited the morning with refreshed energy to continue his journey. He seems to be in good spirits and ready for the challenge, but his attitude has not changed.

The young man seemed to like to do things his own way at his own pace, which is no problem, but what is a problem is the euphoria of the hurrying and competitiveness of getting there first. What do you feel is the precipitating factor that fuels this young man's energy into thinking that he has to be first, that he has all the answers, without relying on sound advice from others? His motivation is remarkable, and his ability to adapt to the environment is somewhat there, but his willingness to accept feedback was lacking. The following page will allow you to ponder on questions to see what is going on with this young man.

Questions

What happens when we try to do things our own way?

23. Think of a time in which you made a decision on your own. What was the outcome of this decision? As believers, we are to pray to God for discernment as to what path to take. Why do we need to consult with God first? Are you open to the suggestions of others? Do you feel like you have to compete with others? How do you feel when others are competing against you? Do you feel like being right all the time? We don't have all the answers. Sometimes someone else may have more experience that can provide more insight. Do you agree with this statement? If so, why? If not, why?

_____

_____

_____

_____

_____

_____

_____

_____

_____

_____

_____

_____

_____

God Provides Warning

God provides us with warnings in subtle and creative ways. If we maintain our closeness to his presence through prayers. We can then receive through his small voice, thunder warnings, or hear him softly speaking guidance and reassurance. Thus alerting us to what lies ahead. No matter what, God loves His children enough to let them know when there is danger. "A man's conscience, like a warning line on the highway, tells him what he shouldn't do - but it does not keep him from doing it." —Frank A Clark

From the prior chapter, we read that the young man took a shortcut on an unknown road to him. In the entrance to the shortcut, a large post in a tree stated, "Enter at your own risk, but it leads you to the mountain top super fast." Just in case you didn't know, the enemy always uses double-negatives when enticing you to take shortcuts. It's almost as if he is using mockery or trickery. "Beware but come on in any way; you will still get there faster." The enemy uses false illusions to entice you into thinking that what you see is gold, but it is false gold. The young man tried to cut corners and continued to follow the shortcuts which led to other unknown roadways. He will soon find out that perilous roads lead to the top faster but they can become the most dangerous roads. And unwarranted dangers will be faced on every side on the journey. But still on he went, telling himself, "I am not afraid of what may come."

"I will get to the top before the old man." The young man kept telling himself over and over again, "I want to get to the top." As if he was in a competition or race. But why is he in a hurry? They both were heading in the same direction, but he still wanted to get there first and prove his point.

The young man kept going and going through rough areas of swamps full of insects and bugs. These are representative of the spiritual attacks that we set upon ourselves when we are not following our godly purpose. He thought for a second, "This is just a challenge that I will transcend!" The young man bravely said, "I am still not afraid." He thought he knew what he was doing, and unfortunately, he was not prepared for what he was about to see. But little did he know that the perilous road can also become a place in which your life is at risk of dangers.

This type of experience also happens when you are closer to your breakthrough. It just so happens that the enemy sends in more distractions or challenges to try to delay or divert your course or cause barriers, sending you into a perilous situation, dangers, and misleading your path. And when we realize that we made bad choices, it is kind of late to turn back, and we will most likely need to start the process all over again. Pay attention to the warning signs, pay attention to the distractions, and don't lean on your own understanding but seek God to guide you in the process instead. Be prepared to learn difficult lessons because you chose to do it your own way and entered at your own risk. The next page will allow you to reflect on this part of the story to gain insight into how to be prepared to see the warning signs before making a decision.

Questions

God Provides Warning

24. In the prior paragraph, we discussed how it is important to consider God's confirmation in decision making. Do you think that God provides confirmation to us? We understand that when God provides us with confirmation it brings a sense of reassurance and safety. God also provides warning to let you know if you will encounter hardship. How open are you to listen to God's voice? Explain why it is important to be obedient. What is one thing that you can do prior to making a decision and entering at your risk? It is ok to be adventurous and self-reliant but sometimes we have to take a step back and accept guidance. Do you agree with this statement?

_____

_____

_____

_____

_____

_____

_____

_____

_____

_____

_____

_____

Be Careful Who You Let in Your Life as Negative People Will Try to Distract You

We hope that people we love, or that the friends we have, will be happy for us or help us by supporting our dreams. But it is far from reality because, the fact is, that many will come with bad intentions to stop you from achieving your dreams. Some come to discourage you and make you feel like you can't or are not qualified enough to do what God has called you out to do. Then there are some who you know who are able to support you with their expertise or just support your goals but refuse to. These are the ones that suddenly reappear after you have climbed the mountain. Once you are successful, everyone wants to know you, be around you, and/or say they know you. However, when you desperately needed their support, they rejected, ignored, and refused to support you. This is the harsh reality. My encouragement to you is to not depend on anyone but God, as people can fail us.

Now, let's get back to our story... The young man continued on as if he were the king of the road. As he was approaching closer to the end of the road in a dark area and near a swampy lot, he saw what appeared to be a snake, which he attempted to evade. But as quickly as he was trying to evade one that was visually in sight, another snake came from behind in an attempt to strike as others were slowly progressing towards his sides. He was bitten and left for dead. The young man was tired and now ill. Out of breath, he managed to see the silhouette of the old wise man at a far distance, and he tried to scream but did not have any strength left. But, as he caught his breath again, he faintly called for help and yelled out the old man's name.

"Hey can you hear me? I am right here," but silence was all he had felt. Almost giving up hope but yet still he waited and wished for the old man to catch a glimpse of him.

Desperate time calls for desperate measures. Those sneaky snakes come from all sides and may appear convincing. These snakes are a representation of the perils of backstabbers, making bad decisions and their consequences, toxic or negative people. They often come with a hidden agenda which is to cause delay, barriers, or attempt to steal your blessings. Be careful, as this is a dangerous spot to be in because they cause major damages to your business or integrity or engage others to not support you.

On your life journey, you will always encounter jealous people attempting to discourage you. Especially when they see that you keep growing in your business. And the more that you progress or excel in your walk with God and in your business, the more you will encounter spiritual attacks. This is the time in which you need to do more praying and fasting as well as maintaining a calm demeanor. The important thing is to not react and not to engage. The minute you start to try to defend yourself is the minute that they will discredit you in front of others whom they have recruited to join the bandwagon of ruining your reputation. They may try, but God tells us in His word in Isaiah 54:17 that "No weapon formed against us shall prosper." This means that nothing they try to do to hurt you or your business will be effective. This is a reassurance to leave it all in God's hands, and He will take care of the rest and keep you safe. You have to be brave and tell the enemy how big your God is as opposed to allowing the overwhelming attacks make you feel like they have more power. They don't know that your God is the God of miracles and wonders, and He will never leave you nor forsake you. He is there with you even when danger surrounds you.

I want to share this quote as an example of how backstabbing sounds and looks. The quote is by Angelica Hopes.

"True understanding and mutual respect do not bridge blames, destructive, negative criticisms, false excuses, and gossip. To express disappointments and ill-feelings are normal; however, to gossip around certain people and events in order to put another person down and destroy one's credibility is a form of bullying whether one expresses it publicly or privately. Beware of segregation, regionalism, individualism, discrimination, stereotyping, destructive criticism, false accusation, biased wrong assumption, prejudice, senseless comparison, and unwanted competition because life is much more meaningful to live for where there is unity and harmony."

In the following page, you will get to learn more about the topic of "snakes" aka backstabbers. This sounds a bit harsh, but reality is that not everyone is happy to see you progressing in your life.

Questions

Be Careful Who You Let in Your Life as Negative People Will Try to Distract You

25. Whenever you are building something for yourself, you must be careful as to who you allow in your life as not everyone that comes into your life will be happy for you or mean to celebrate with you. Also, be careful who you share your dreams or your plans with. From reading this part of the story, what is your impression? There is a quote that goes like this: "Not everyone is rooting for you; some are just waiting for you to fail." What do you understand by this saying? I am not suggesting being harsh, but to guard your heart and mind, so that the enemy does not steal what is legitimately yours. Do you agree with this statement? If so, what part of it do you agree or disagree with? How do you feel about the topic of snakes or backstabbers? Do they exist? And have you experienced this relationship dynamic? Is it healthy to have the support from others but be discerning about who you let in? And if so, why?

_____

_____

_____

_____

_____

_____

_____

_____

When we Surrender, God Shows Up

Why is it when we are lost, broken, or tried to do everything on our own, we reach a point of brokenness, feeling lost, and in jeopardy? The situation humbles us so deeply that it brings us to our knees. Then God shows up and brings us hope, restores us, and shakes us into the truth of our lives. God comes in at a nick of time to let us know that He can restore us even when we have failed. It is in this humbling experience that we find ourselves in a desperate situation asking for God's help when we should have allowed Him to work in our lives from the first time that we took a bad turn.
—Claribel Coreano

The old, wise man, upon seeing the young man hurt and lifeless, came running to his aid and asked the young man what happened. The young man quickly explained that a snake had bitten his hands and another bitten him in his back. The meaning of the bites on the hands is from those who are close to us who sometimes covertly do not want us to succeed, and those from behind are friends, acquaintances, people you know, and sometimes even strangers who are jealous, and you have no idea why. The ones to your side are other fellow business owners who love to compete with you and deter your progress because they feel intimidated by your accomplishments, turning what could have been a productive networking relationship into a needless toxic reaction. To expand it a little bit more, there are individuals who come close enough to find out and see what you are working on as opposed to asking "Hey, can we schedule a meeting, so we chat and exchange ideas" or "I see that you are good at this, can we meet so that you can show me on how you do this." Perhaps the person is great at marketing "asking them if they need some help in this area," it does not have to be giving them your whole toolbox but at least guiding them the right way. I like to teach, motivate, and encourage others, and if you ask me, "Can I use your quote that you posted yesterday?" I will without thinking twice tell them, "Yes, by all means." For one, the person has demonstrated respect to you as an individual by taking the time to ask. It also shows that they value and admire your materials.

They are also showing that they are supportive of others, and this is a good thing because they want others to grow not only personally but in their business. The reason is that you never know if the person that you are asking will become successful, and you may need their expertise again. The analogy of the snakes could be just about anything in your life that creates resistance towards your purpose or vision.

The old wise man said to the young man, "You know, you could have prevented all this! If you would have at least listened and taken the advice from this old wise man." You see, the old man had taken these same roads before and learned from all of his mistakes to know the safest and most secured roads. The old man knew what to expect and how to protect himself in case he encountered any snakes. Lessons learned help you use more precaution in order to prevent further pain, distractions, and unsafe relationships that may cause you delays or barriers.

In fact, the old wise man had successfully climbed to the top of the mountain several times before. And although he never took any shortcuts, he already knew that if you took shortcuts you may get there faster, but risk your life and all the work you had already put in with no guarantee that you would make it out alive every time. The old wise man had been prepared, and he carried the antidote that would save this young man's life. When he got near the young man, he did not ask any questions because he knew what he had to do. He gave him the antidote without the young man even asking for it. The antidote in this case is the realization of conviction of what the young man did and the ability to reflect on his mistakes by reading the Bible, praying, and getting into God's presence as He will always keep you safe and protected. The old man had gained discernment through the lessons he had learned. The main lesson he learned is to not make the same mistakes again or allow the enemy to convince you to take shortcuts. No matter how enticing, easy, or available everything looks. It's about building a strong foundation through the applications of the lessons learned that will then make it easier for things to flow with ease even if it takes you longer than others. Whenever you are faced with this type of situation, think about this story.

When the young man came around, he regretfully and solemnly told the old wise man, "Thank you for saving my life. I should have listened to your advice; it would have saved me from this setback." I learned that I am not always right and that sometimes I have to take a step back to reflect on godly and human guidance for feedback from others. I learned that you could never be too sure of the paths because directions often change, and your plans may change as well. I learned that there is always a preparation time that equips you with the tools you need for the journey. This is why it is always good to take your time and be at your pace. As long as you're making progress you will still get there to the pinnacle of success as long as you remain steady and committed to getting to where you are headed. And always remember not to listen to the opinions of how others think what you should already be in or have accomplished. Your journey is your journey, not theirs. Like this young man, in this story, who tried to live up to the expectations of others by getting to the top right away. This not only sets ourselves up for failures but also makes us start over. This is when you have to regain your inner self-strength and validate your progress and accomplishments.

As he regained his strength, they then both got up and continued on the road and the old wise man asked the young man, "Hey, you never answered my question. What do you think is the most important thing in life?" The following questions will help you reflect on situations in which you made decisions that affected your life. Jesus always saves us at the right time when we least expect it. He never leaves us nor forsakes us.

Questions

When We Surrender, God Shows Up

26. God comes into our lives in a nick of time to pick us up every time we fail. Can you remember a time in your life in which you felt broken, lost, or unsafe? Or when you made horrible decisions that affected your life? What did you do to turn your life around? How did you come out of the situation or feelings? What do you think is the most important thing in life? What do you do when you are faced with a tough situation in which you have to make a decision that can either break you or make you better? Who do you rely on?

_____

_____

_____

_____

_____

_____

_____

_____

_____

_____

_____

_____

_____

_____

_____

_____

_____

_____

_____

_____

_____

_____

_____

_____

_____

_____

_____

_____

_____

_____

_____

_____

_____

_____

_____

A Lesson Learned Hurts but Brings Awareness

*If we don't reflect or do introspection within to explore and analyze
what we learned from the lesson, we will not grow from it. It is
important to be open to correction and use it as a growth tool. This
same tool God will allow it to be used for a testimony. "There are
certain life lessons that you can only learn in the struggle."*
—Idowu Koyenikan

The young man looked perplexed in thought and said, "You must not rush in the journey or attempt to take shortcuts to the top. You must walk along the right path that will take you there safe and sound and not in a flash. Patience and timing are the key! God's timing is priority because we can't get ahead of God's schedule or allow delays. The decisions you make will determine if you are happy or not! Because you could easily lose yourself in the climb. The dangers can jeopardize your health or risk you not getting there at all. Everyone's pace is different; the journey may take longer but what matters is what you do to get there and what you do once you reach the top as well as what you do afterwards.

"I learned that listening to the advice of an old wise man (mentor or godly counsel) is a golden nugget that will always be treasured inside my heart." Remembering that it is not the person's appearance or influence that solely matters, but the message that they are offering to you with good intentions that will help you grow in life and in business.

The old wise man said to the young man in response, "We all, at one point or another, wanted to reach the mountain top as fast as we could, without thinking of the perilous dangers of the different roads ahead.

Like you said, it's best to climb at your own pace, no shortcuts, no head bumping in the road that will get you there safely. There is enough room for everyone to get there at their own pace, with their own skills, and with their own motivation. Listen to this wise old man - I have been there and done that, and it wasn't until I faced dangers myself that I realized that I made a mistake and learned from it. I now know all the secrets to tell others when they begin their journey to their climb! Don't live life in a hurried pace—appreciate everything around you—love with all your heart and always, always put God first in all you travel in your journey. You will get there but in time with God's aligning! This is what's important in everyone's life journey! Having goals and being ambitious is fine as long as it doesn't take away from your valuable time with your loved ones or taking care of yourself and maintaining your health.

"Being wealthy or rich is fine too, as long as you don't idolize money." Again reflecting on Steve Jobs who stated, "Non-stop pursuit of wealth will only turn a person into a twisted being, just like me" (snopes.com) and "Being the richest man in the cemetery doesn't matter to me. Going to bed at night saying we've done something wonderful...that's what matters to me." Both these quotes deliver a self-discovery message that Steve Jobs realized; however, for him it was too late as he was already on his deathbed. The time accumulating wealth can't be reversed because the time spent caused him his health. I am sharing these quotes as reminders that the most valuable things in your life are your health and how you spend your time. The concept of money is not bad but idolizing it is.

Remember that money is not the root of all evil but the love of it is. 1 Timothy 6:10, "For the love of money is a root of all kinds of evils. It is through this craving that some have wandered away from the faith and pierced themselves with many snake bites pangs." The moment you idolize money, it becomes your God, and you lose the passion you once had and the reason you wanted to start the business in the first place. For example, never forget that if you started your business to help people - that should be your daily mantra. It is not going to bring you the same sense of accomplishment you used to get. Once you adapt to this type of mindset, you will see everything fall in its place. The doors of blessing will open up and overflow with financial blessings because you are now aligned with gratitude, purpose, and helping others.

The following questions will help you explore experiences you had in which you went through situations that raised awareness in you and helped you become more accountable in your life. The best way that we can develop and grow is by conducting inner self-healing by exploring experiences we may have not known were life lessons. Knowing where your focus is determines where it will take you. Always remember that the goal is not only to create a successful business that is financially sustainable but also one that leaves an impact on the lives of others. Your aim is to build a business that has integrity and is known for the quality of service provided to its clients, and if the clients are happy with your services, they will refer others to your business. The next page will give you an opportunity to explore gaining awareness through lessons learned.

Questions

A Lesson Learned Hurts but Brings Awareness

27. Can you think of a lesson that you have experienced that brought you a sense of awareness? Are you open to doing a thorough introspection of yourself? What areas of your life do you need to address, correct, and change? Are you open to doing the work? It's not easy, but you have to be willing to explore some areas of your life that can bring painful feelings in order to heal completely - you must acknowledge the wounds.

_____

_____

_____

_____

_____

_____

_____

_____

_____

_____

_____

_____

_____

_____

What Can We Take from This Story?

Are there any patterns that you identify with? How do you feel about "lessons learned?" So, what is the most important thing in your life? And why? What do you feel is the message from this story? What resonates in your heart and mind? Do you feel like you can identify with the story?

This quote by Rasheed Oguntaru speaks volumes. "While you'll feel compelled to charge forward, it's often a gentle step back that will reveal to you where you are and what you truly seek," Taking a step back not only allows that space to reflect where you are, but also to explore any setbacks, and also evaluate what you learned from the experiences. What can you do to move forward now that you have reached a sense of awareness about that lesson learned?

The moral of this story is that life is a journey that we all get to experience and then reach an end, and it doesn't matter what we did, accomplished, or how much money we made but how we lived our lives. Were we being present or were doing so much that we were absent, instead of enjoying the special moments of life? In Ecclesiastes 2:11, "Then I looked at all the works that my hands had done And on the labor in which I had toiled, And indeed all was vanity and grasping for the wind." There was no profit under the sun. Solomon, in all his accomplishments, found the answer to the most important thing in life. At the end of that climb to the highest mountain, Solomon realized that it was all Vanity. This word in Hebrew means vapor, and it is reflecting on how quickly life passes by and how everything, even the good things, also pass. Solomon refers to it as "They were grasping for the wind." Solomon is not saying that having a good life is bad, but what you do with that good life is what is most valuable. Solomon understood that he reached a pinnacle of wisdom and riches in which he felt so comfortable that he forgot that God was the one that had blessed him.

Solomon turned away from God and worshiped other idols, thus sinning against God. He became distant from God. Solomon became distracted by the snakes that came to divert his beliefs, morals, and values by adapting to his wife's belief systems of idol worship. Solomon knew that while he had everything he wanted and all the riches of the world, nothing could compare to the peace and contentment he had when he was honoring God. And this meaningless feeling that he felt came as a result of him distancing himself from God. At his lowest point in life, he had already been bitten by the snake, and he found himself in a dark place due to the separation from God's presence. He is warning us to pay attention that we don't allow the riches of this world to distance us from God because, after all, everything becomes meaningless.

Solomon knew that having God and being the center of it all was what made it all possible for him to be able to make wise decisions by exercising the wisdom God had anointed him with. And like that old wise man, he knows what is good for us. In Proverbs 14:13, Solomon wrote that even in the pleasures of life. He describes it as sheer madness. "Even in laughter the heart may know sorrow, and the end of mirth may be grief." No one is spared from bad times. Pleasure seeking leads to grief. Solomon was using self-reflection to teach this important lesson, which is that knowing what is important early on in life is more valuable than everything you have gained or accumulated because at the end of the road, when life's journey ends, you will not take it with you. Solomon knew that all too well as he disobeyed God in his later years. He was the richest man in the land, even having everything and knowing that God blessed him, but he turned his back on God, and this is why he thought of life as meaningless. There was now a separation between him and God due to his sin. He did not find himself worthy of forgiveness nor did he ask God for it. At this point, he was like the young man - left lifeless and almost dying due to the bites. Solomon was experiencing a spiritual death by the separation from the source.

Remember that being rich is a state of mind; you can be rich in health, rich with a healthy family, rich in love given by others, rich in what you give others, and rich in having a relationship with your creator. "Rich" is wholeness in life, maintaining goodness in your soul, doing good to others, respecting life, and respecting others. In short, it is the richness of your character, how you love others, and how you treat others that make you worth more than what a billionaire is worth. The balance tilts when you step in it. Although God does not want to see us in poverty either, He desires for us to be blessed and as long as we are loyal to Him, meaning seeking His presence first in every decision is imperative. Having that ability to stay motivated, trusting in God in the process, staying calm and patient when waiting on God, is powerful. We will become rich in character, and this is where the balance lies. Desiring inner growth is worth more than many worldly things because whatever you have, God can bless it to become more and more. This means that whatever you create, own, or do for His glory and praise, He will bless you with His favor, and this ensures that everything grows. But you must give back to others, and His blessings will multiply. In the following page, you will have the opportunity to explore some questions that will help you gain more insight into the story and reflect on your take and how you can apply it to your own journey.

Questions

What can we take from this story?

28. Now that you have read this short story, what's your take on the story? Are there any patterns that you see? Can you relate to any part of this story? If so, how and why? What can you learn from Solomon's Ecclesiastes 2:11? "Then I looked at all the work that my hands had done And on the labor in which I had toiled; And indeed, all was vanity and grasping for the wind. There was no profit under the sun." What reflection can we extract from the wisdom of this verse?

_____

_____

_____

_____

_____

_____

_____

_____

_____

_____

_____

_____

_____

_____

_____

_____

Better Life, Better Health, Better Mindset

Having a positive mindset helps you maintain your mind free of clutter and negativity and propels you to live better and focus on your health so that you can accomplish your dreams. If you are not taking care of yourself, your health, and what you feed your mind, this will affect your focus, direction, and motivation. So, if you want to have a better life, better health, and a better mindset, then you must take care of all these areas in order to maintain a balance. There is a quote by Debbie Hampton that goes like this: "Take care of your mind, your body will thank you. Take care of your body, your mind will thank you." We see that health is wealth and more valuable than money; having health is being wealthy. It is needed in order to be able to work on your dreams and goals.

I heard a saying that goes like this: "Don't forget God when you get what you prayed for." What this statement is saying is that God needs to be honored because he has blessed us with a better life, better health, and better mindset. When you work on your healing, you have to work in all areas of your life that have been affected by it. If you want to gain or achieve a better life, health, and mindset, you must empty the vessel from all the baggage carried from all the years of holding unhealed parts of your life. Understand that God's mercy and Grace will help you achieve your healing. But you must desire to be healed, and you must be willing to work on being healed and also open to change from the old to the new.

It first starts with changing any negative mindsets that have affected you for so long and changing them to a more positive mindset. You will be strong enough to face every challenge or struggle with more strength and determination. This will create a stronger sense of resilience in your being. Take care of every area of your life to create better health and a healthier mindset because you know you are equipped and have the resources to follow and live a better life. It's achievable! Adapting to a healthier and more positive mindset requires changing behaviors and habits, and adapting to life coping skills that will enhance your life and get rid of those behaviors that affect your growth. It is going to require soul-searching for inner core issues that have kept you trapped in negative thinking. Then, you will need to acknowledge them, identify them, and label them. Forgive yourself and then let them go. It is an important part of the process of healing and must be completed in order to heal those areas of your life that have created barriers, obstacles, or self-sabotaging behaviors. On the following page, you will have the opportunity to explore ways in which you can improve your life, improve your health, and improve your mindset. It is important to take time for self-care and time alone to reflect and rest.

Questions

Better Life, Better Health, Better Mindset

29. Name one thing that you can change in your life that will improve your health and wellbeing. Having a positive mindset is important in self-care - what do you do for yourself to help you in maintaining a positive mindset? What do you do when you feel overwhelmed? When the past comes knocking at your door, what do you do? Do you believe that healing is an ongoing process? If so, why? Are you able to have self-compassion for yourself? How do you demonstrate it?

_____

_____

_____

_____

_____

_____

_____

_____

_____

_____

_____

_____

_____

_____

_____

_____

_____

_____

_____

_____

_____

_____

_____

_____

_____

_____

_____

_____

_____

_____

_____

_____

_____

_____

Keeping Up with the Momentum

Why is it important to keep up with the momentum? Learning how to balance your responsibilities at home and in your new career, dream, or business is important because it will determine the degree of balance each demands. This helps with keeping yourself motivated, feeling restored, and in maintaining your vision. What can you do to maintain your momentum? "The rhythm of daily action aligned with your goals creates the momentum that separates dreamers from super-achievers." —Darren Hardy

It is important to keep up with the momentum. This happens when you learn to balance all areas of your life according to what is being expected of you. Let's say for instance that the demands are greater than the time you have to provide for yourself. Then, you must evaluate a balanced medium in this area, for if you give too much of yourself without taking care of your overall well being, it can result in burnout or giving too much of yourself, putting you at risk of becoming a people pleaser. Reaching the momentum is when you are able to say no when no is required and yes when you are available and ready to give. The momentum is like a pendulum that moves by taking back and moving forward back to you, not swaying just in one direction, but a steady movement of transfer and of receiving in order to be able to give back more of yourself. It is a balancing act of give and take because you do not want to give too much of yourself, allowing it to deplete you because you can not give or nurture if your cup is empty. Thus you need to learn how to reach this balance because if you tend to be a perfectionist or workaholic like me, it will certainly take a toll not only on your life but your health. It may not have visible effects right away, but it will catch up with you later in life.

Keeping up with the momentum means a happy life by creating time for your loved ones and balancing both your business and family. Keeping yourself motivated will demand a commitment to taking better care of yourself spiritually, physically, and mentally. This is needed to be able to balance your home life, relationship with God, and your business. Maintaining momentum means that you will keep yourself walking in the light with spiritual discernment to know what decisions you must make and what people you are going to allow in your business. Balancing everything is like a juggling act, but with the right organization, patience, and calm, it is achievable.

Another way to take care of yourself is to make more time available or manage your time for your business well. There are many ways you can do this. For example, you can use appointment apps to schedule clients. You can also use task manager like Friday, Toggl, or Trello and many other apps available. You can keep a task organizer blackboard to write down your appointments and follow-ups. You can keep an Excel sheet with all of your contacts' names, addresses, and phone numbers for easier access. If your business is already thriving, you may want to hire an administrative assistant to keep you on track with everything and help you provide the best customer services support to ensure clients continue to be engaged and stay happy with your services. The important thing is to manage your business effectively and dedicate your personal time for self-care. It becomes easier to manage the daily routine tasks, and it will translate into extra time available to tackle the difficult tasks and concentrate on creating more leads, engaging clients, and completing the financial part of the business to ensure that bills are paid on a timely basis. The next page will allow you to explore how you feel about maintaining your business thriving and reaching a momentum of balance in your business.

Questions

Keeping Up with the Momentum

30. Ok, so you started your business, and it is thriving and stable. How do you keep up with the momentum to keep yourself grounded? How do you balance your responsibilities at home, business, career, goals, and relationships? How do you achieve balance? Name one thing that you do for yourself to relax and stay motivated. Name a strategy that you have used in the past that has helped you stay organized with your finances, homelife, and/or business.

_____

_____

_____

_____

_____

_____

_____

_____

_____

_____

_____

_____

Stay on Track by Reinventing Yourself Daily

You must reinvent yourself daily to be able to keep fresh ideas or creativity at its peak. In order to keep yourself and your business competitive in the market, keeping up with all the marketing, social media, and other trends is necessary to stand out in your local community as well as nationally and internationally. "Every day you reinvent yourself. You're always in motion. But you decide every day: forward or backward." —James Altucher

Have you heard of how authors face a period of "writer's block" which places them in stagnation or perhaps the sense of running out of creativity? This also applies to coaches, encouragers, and artists. You need to reinvent yourself on a daily basis by taking care of your wellness and staying grounded in prayers and in God's word to be able to give back to others with a fresh perspective, clear voice, and message. As a coach, it is recommended that you sign up for a continued education to stay abreast with all the new coaching strategies (and also it is required by many life coaching accreditation schools as part of your ongoing certification). There are several online training websites that offer life coaches continued ed credit courses. One that I have used is Udemy amongst many others. There are also other specialty trainings for coaches like the DISC program to be certified in conducting personality-style coaching programs. Attending training to upgrade your skills, whether it is in coaching, business administration, finances, or human resources will keep your business competitive with other trends. Also, not only training for your business but attending Christian conferences, training, workshops, and/or retreats will allow you an opportunity to network with others, brainstorm ideas, and obtain support. Learning new technology as it changes every two years is essential, and you will need to be competitive to be able to stay current with all business trends.

Another suggestion is to obtain business coaching to keep you abreast of new trends, manage your business effectively, and have a sounding board to discuss challenges. You also can receive life coaching from another coach as it is highly recommended to keep you grounded and healed to continue working on your own healing journey. Sometimes, a coach needs a fresh perspective. A life coach can help you in many different ways. One way is to obtain clarity from any challenges that you are going through, offer you suggestions for your business, and have a good understanding of what to expect from clients and from yourself. Having a coach can also help you when you want to rebrand your business to give it a facelift and re-announce your business with the new branding. This is another way to keep up with the social media trends and make your business more competitive in that arena. Like everything else in life, things get old, and sometimes a logo may work for a few years but then lose its luster and attractiveness. You may need to revamp not only your branding and logo but perhaps clarify your vision, mission, and business principles. In the following page, you will have an opportunity to explore more in detail the topic of reinventing yourself in many different ways.

Questions

Stay on Track by Reinventing Yourself Daily

31. To continue to thrive in your business, career, or relationships, you must continuously reinvent yourself to keep up with the culture, trends, and relationship phases. We are not suggesting continuously changing yourself to accommodate what's happening around you but to reinvent yourself for you and your business and continue to be competitive as well as gain a new population of clients. How do you keep yourself open-minded to change? What does reinventing yourself mean to you? If you have ever had experience reinventing yourself, what did it bring you, how did you feel, and how did you do it? What was the outcome or what did you achieve?

_____

_____

_____

_____

_____

_____

_____

_____

_____

_____

_____

_____

What's Next?

Finding an area of expertise is important, and this is found through exploration of your gifts, talents, experiences, and career history. Evaluating what you are good or best at. What is something that you do extremely well that you can teach others? What can you contribute to others? What experience do you have that you can use to help others grow? Do you gear to a specific specialty? Let's say collaborating with women who have experienced trauma, domestic violence, empowering women, or corporate and business coaching.

As a coach, you need to find your niche, and what specialty you bring to the table that others don't offer. What are you good at or have experience of? It could be a topic or something that you have overcome or survived. Think of how you are going to present it to the world and when. What is it that makes you a leader in presenting this topic? What did you learn from it that others may benefit from? How can it help others? Why is it important to share this with others? Know how to gain the trust of the viewers, listeners, or participants. What is your style, your approach, and what kind of perspective do you have that will connect with others? Voice your intentions of what you are trying to accomplish and how you are going to help or present the topics. Here are some tips to help you to understand what to look for, what to expect, and how it matches with your niche:

- Set clear intentions and motives. Be transparent so that they can feel validated, heard, and supported.
- You have to start somewhere; therefore, you need to help others to start building clientele, credibility, and networking.
- Once you have built your tribe, set a standard of how you are going to get paid. Know your audience and target clients. What

are they looking for? What do you have that you can only provide them with that service?

- Empathetically ask the right questions to engage them in your services as they will be more apt to build trust and rapport as a coach/client relationship.
- Have a short elevator speech or audio business card to sell your services to the clients so that they know what you offer and to see if you are a good fit for them as well as for you.
- Not every client will be a good fit.
- You are going to encounter difficult clients as well as challenging clients.
- You set the tone and establish boundaries with them.
- You want to find the right, paying clients. You want to help others, but you also have to maintain your business.

Like any new business owner, it takes time to become a master of selling your business to the clients so that they can buy into and invest their money by paying for their services. It takes practice and more practice until you master it. You are almost completed with this learning journey, and now it's time to think of how the clients will benefit from your services.

Questions

What's Next?

32. You have reached the point at which you have completed a thorough exploration of your strengths, weaknesses, self-expectations, personality, interests, etc. Now is the time to look into your talents, experiences, and career history. What are you good at? What sets you apart from others? What can you contribute to others? What experience do you have that you can use to help others grow? Name those areas and on a piece of paper write down how you envision yourself helping them. How will they benefit from your services? If you can think of a perfect client that you would like to coach, how will they present to you? What tool or technique will you use to assist them?

_____

_____

_____

_____

_____

_____

_____

_____

_____

_____

_____

_____

Effective Marketing Skills

Marketing, social media, and many other platforms are vital in marketing your business. Gaining knowledge of which platforms to use will be most beneficial to your business. Learning how to properly advertise your business or expose your business to top-notch algorithms so that it can automatically market your business is vital in today's social media market. The more knowledge that you acquire on social media platforms, the more it will be an asset for your business. In addition, creating an attractive website is just as important. An attractive, organized, and detailed website will speak for itself and catch the attention of the viewers. Clients will engage because they believe in the described services. Effective marketing skills will bring you the right clients to your website and also advertise your business effectively.

As a beginner, we all learn by trial and error when it comes to marketing. But unless you hire a professional to do all of your marketing, you will struggle with having to take extra time to create posts, videos, and other media responses which can also take from your available time of providing services to clients and managing other aspects of the business. You, as the business owner, will need to make sure to take time to market your business and make videos and announcements amongst many other media-related marketing strategies. These are also time-consuming because you will need time to edit, revise, and sometimes redo videos. One way you can start marketing your business is by getting involved in some Facebook Groups with like-minded life coaches to start networking and sharing your services. Here are some tips on how to start.

- Be a guest blogger. Sign up to be interviewed by business network groups and be consistent with your social media by learning the ropes of what makes an effective social media platform.

- Start podcasting, being consistent, and showing up. Creating a social media presence will help attract the right clients who will want your services and believe in what you offer.

- Podcasting takes discipline, commitment, and excellent organizational skills. It is a process of engaging new monthly guests, following up with emails, confirming dates/times via Calendly as well as confirming topics.

- Know that some guests may want to get to know you first and learn more about the podcast thus requesting a pre-meeting.

- Be prepared for the actual day of the podcast appointment. You have to make sure that all of your equipment is set up and your Zoom link is working properly or any other podcasting video recording apps that you may want to use.

- After your podcast appointment you have to dedicate time to edit your video and, once edited, upload it to all social media and Spotify as an audio version.

- The last process is an email to your guests thanking them and also letting them know where to find all uploads of the video by providing them with all social media links.

- Email marketing: Once you are established in social media, start your email marketing newsletters by offering different life coaching topics, tips, or workshops.

- Being consistent and creative is what attracts attention to your business, website, and other social media apps that you use.

- Create a schedule of what day during the week you will send the newsletter if it is a monthly or quarterly newsletter. You want to simplify your life and a monthly newsletter may be productive. The same with the marketing emails you may choose 2 or 3 days during the week on which to send the email, again you want to be productive but not overwhelm the receivers with so many emails that they unsubscribe.

- Lastly, learn about how other coaches do it and ask how it has been working for them. For example, If you hire a marketing person they will develop a marketing strategy on how they are going to outreach and what keywords they will use to attract traffic and also affect the algorithm to disperse your information to new prospective clients.

- Build an online community by using videos to attract clients, provide a service, or teach a free workshop to start showing your presence in the life coaching arena. Network with other coaches to build a consistent referral system and support.

- Do a group coaching online or in person by teaching a class or conducting a coaching session on a topic of interest.

- Optimize your social media group engagement, let's say in a live session on YouTube or TikTok. Post reels on Instagram that are consistent with your coaching business services. Use your current database to attract more clients and network your business.

Now, let's talk about the technology aspect of the business.

- If you are currently constructing your website, make sure to manage it attentively. If you have hired a developer, you want them to construct it based on your services, your personality, and what you are selling, not their own style.

- Stay on top of things by being consistent with writing your content, making sure you are keeping it updated, and creating new content to keep the clients engaged and continuously engaging new clients.

- Spend time in places where you can engage potential clients. Have an elevator pitch ready to engage conversations or, as my business coach likes to call it, "an audio business card" that works more effectively.

- Leverage your experience by knowing your worth, what you offer, and what you bring to the table. Knowing your worth is important because it sets the standard for the quality of services that you provide along with expertise and knowledge. You work hard to become a life coach, don't settle for less than what you feel you are worth. Set the standard that what you offer is valuable and worth the price you're asking for.

- You have the right to turn away people who may not qualify for your type of coaching, or who may not need what you offer. It is ok to tell them: "It doesn't sound like I am a good fit for the services that I offer, and what you need is not my niche. However, I can refer you to someone who does."

- Be ok with saying no to someone who does not want to commit or acts like they don't need your services, or who may not be willing to pay for the services.

- Any professional life coach with integrity will be strong enough to pass off a client opportunity rather than take their money just to make money off the person when you know right off the bat they do not fit with the services or what you offer. This is your integrity that you place on the line because while the client was not a good match for your services you took their money when they could have been benefiting from services from another coach that matched what they needed. Let them go, no money is worth losing your integrity and credibility over bad customer service. In this world of complaints, social media exposure, and sue-happy individuals, it's better to lose one client than to risk it.

- You want clients that are committed to not only paying for their services but committed to making changes because they match the services that you offer.

- Know who are the clients you are looking for to provide services to. In other words, know your niche. For example, create a short mission statement that includes a short paragraph on the kind of people you want to provide services to, detailing demographics, a target population, and how they are going to benefit from the services. Describe the actual benefits and how it would look like for the person as well as how it is going to help them grow. Provide them with a brighter future or inspire their own story of hope or moving forward.

Marketing is your spotlight needed for your business to be discovered, and connecting with the right people is important. Finding the right marketing services is a priority. Knowing that they have your vested interests at hand to help you shine not because they want to make money out of you but because if you shine, their business will be highlighted. Your business will help market their own business as a successful record of accomplishment. The right marketing person will guide you to the right marketing strategy, branding to reach your marketing goals, branding, and events. It will happen with a flow of blessings. Aim for consistency, coordination, and meaning so that it all correlates with the services you will be providing or are providing.

Questions

Effective Marketing Skills

33. What social media outlets are you familiar with? Does social media come easy to you, or do you need additional knowledge? How much do you know about marketing in social media? What do you feel is the best approach to use in marketing your business? How comfortable do you feel with social media, making videos, or podcasting? Can you envision yourself making a video or being a guest on a podcast? What will be your topic? How will you get prepared? What important message do you hope to share with the viewers?

_____

_____

_____

_____

_____

_____

_____

_____

_____

_____

_____

_____

_____

Branding

What is your branding? What themes, logos, and/or areas of focus do you familiarize yourself with? It can be a quote, a symbol, or anything else that speaks loudly of what you represent, what you offer, and how you are offering it. Why is branding important? It is important because it is a tool that attracts clients to your website, business cards, and brochures. It has to be personable; color coding and strong, catchy fonts are just as important as making sure to choose the right color palette flows uniformly because it represents you and your company. You want an attention-catching logo, something that people will remember and anyone who sees it will associate with your business.

Who are your ideal clients? Let's say for example you want to work with women with a past history of domestic violence or self-esteem issues. Identify what they will achieve through your services. Describe what makes them ready to receive the services, the level of commitment, and how they will need to become open to change behaviors. Why would they want a coach like yourself to help them? Know what you can do for them or how you will help them overcome a history of domestic violence or self-esteem issues, etc. It is important to become the coach you would want to hire, offering the services that you would seek from a life coach. What your business offers should align with what you would want to receive as a coach.

Evaluating and conducting introspection: why do you want to help this population? Do you really do it to help others? Or are you visualizing a lucrative money-making business first? I saw a video two years ago about one of the greatest life coaches in the United States. I don't remember his name, but his story was so impactful and left a good impression on me. He said that his earnings were beyond what you and I ever heard someone make as a coach and that is what he earns in the present. He mentioned the mantra that he lives by is, "I coach to help people." He says that he has never diverted from this mantra and that he did not allow money to be his priority. He said the money will eventually flow because you are making a difference in people's lives. He explained that they were his best promoters, by word of mouth, because they shared their own testimonials with others and told others how he made a difference in their lives, therefore, bringing him more clients. This is what made his business successful, and he became known for this exceptional executive coaching.

Executive coaching is a higher level of coaching that involves working directly with CEOs/CFOs of Fortune 500 executives who are seeking the guidance of a business or the organizational structure of the business. The life coach helps them with managing their corporations, businesses, or financial companies by teaching them emotional intelligence, leadership skills, staff management, and how to create a positive culture of the company as well as implement risk management practices. This is a top priority for any company or business, and to explain how important risk management is for any company, business, or corporation, we must know what it means. The term "risk" is defined as "the effects of uncertainty in an agency or company objectives." If policies and procedures are not written down or clearly defined, there is room for misrepresentation or liabilities, thus resulting in gray areas that can become a risk factor. The term "risk management" is defined as "the process of evaluating activities and processes to direct and control the organization's risks or liabilities." An evaluation process should always be practiced as this allows the organization transparency and the opportunity to find out the areas where risk has been identified to properly address them. This process applies to not just policy and procedures but the whole company as well as all departments including any programming, development, and client satisfaction. It is highly effective and productive for any CEOs/CFOs or company presidents to obtain this high-level guidance, especially if they are new in their roles or replacing someone else who has left the company. A life coach can help the executive set goals for the company based on how he or she intends to improve areas of deficiencies that they have inherited from past leadership. But, going back to the life coach experience, whether it is a high-level leadership client, a blue-collar worker, or a person who is just struggling with life issues, they are just as important.

In order to know your branding, you must know what population you are interested in serving and feel equipped to share your wisdom and expertise. Where can you find this client population? Knowing this will help with marketing the services appropriately. How is your coaching different? What makes you stand out? What is it about you that other coaches do not possess or provide? You are unique; your story, experiences, and what you bring to the table help engage the right people. Think of what your branding will be, sound like, or look like. Does it represent you in every way, shape, or form? Does it represent your values, beliefs, and the message you want to convey? Is it catching the right colors, and does it represent what you want the world to know? Put on your thinking cap because the next page will have some interesting questions that will help you evaluate what your branding will represent to you.

Questions

Branding

34. Your branding represents you, your business, values, style, and unique representation of the services that you offer. Make a list of positive adjectives that describe you, business, style, writing, communication, etc. How important is it to have the right branding package? Having a unique logo represents your company and also provides a snippet of what you are all about. Think of different pictures that send a message about the business that you want to create. What does the picture look like? Think of different typesetting fonts that you would like to use that match your branding. What do you want your business cards to look like? Remember that everything has to be customized to match your branding uniformly.

_____

_____

_____

_____

_____

_____

_____

_____

_____

_____

Online Presence and Social Media

Your online presence is important. What are you trying to portray online? Does it match up to your values, morals, and spiritual beliefs? Does it match the services that you provide? Do you feel like it engages the viewers? Do you feel comfortable in your own skin? Are you open to making videos or being a guest in a podcast or interview? Do you follow the social media trends? Do you create your own trends?

Again, this is where your marketing campaign comes into play. What are you bringing to the World Wide Web that is different and engaging to people? Why should they choose to seek your services? What do you offer that is different from others? The important thing is for the viewers to know and understand that the focus is to provide quality services that promote personal growth in whatever area in which you are providing services. After all, that is the most valuable aspect of your image. Be the light … be that focus … be the change of catalyst that others need. Be you … be different. Your originality and genuineness is what will bring them to trust you. The minute you change that and try to be like everyone else, you lose their trust and interest. Sometimes, we see what others are doing and we want to try it to see if it works for us, but I am one that will encourage you not to do so. Being original feels more comfortable for me; it will be too stressful to try to adapt to what others are presenting themselves with. I will totally feel like an imposter because I am not a follower. I feel more comfortable with my quirks, imperfections, and weirdness. But that is me! My question to you is what will help you build that online presence, credibility, and success?

The most important thing to remember is that your online presence is your selling point, and it has to be creative, attractive, and able to monetize your selling products. Monetize all of your digital products. Facebook can be a great advertising platform to assist in creating other venues of networking and gaining clients. You also can promote your Facebook content to reach more followers the same way you can do on Instagram. You can also sell a physical product, let's say a logo on T-shirts, cups, handbags, coaching books, or self-help session downloads. You can have a storefront that also offers affiliate products from other people. You should advertise your coaching services. If you conduct non-profit consulting, sell your self-help books. They should be advertised on your website, and promotional materials should be made available. Advertise hosting live events and calendars and join Patreon to build and promote your business more independently. Start thinking about how you would like your social media to look, then answer the questions on the following page.

Questions

Online Presence and Social Media

35. Your online presence is important. What you are trying to portray online has to match up with your business, branding language, and communication. Does it match up to your values, morals, and spiritual beliefs? Do you feel like it engages the viewers? Do you feel comfortable in your skin? Or do you follow other people's trends? Make sure that all platforms match together to your website and branding package. How likely are you to hire a marketing coach? If very likely, what will be the selling point that will help you hire them?

_____

_____

_____

_____

_____

_____

_____

_____

_____

_____

_____

_____

Maintaining and Managing

*Every business needs to make sure that they can attain
sustainability. Having the appropriate business-related software is
essential. For example, payment methods platforms like PayPal,
Square, cash apps, or other credit card software.
A budgeting software to keep track of payments and all expenses
and creating a budget plan that includes sustainability for the
future are also key.*

If you have a home office, make sure that you have adequate equipment to function in an office including computers, printers, screens, microphones, or other electronic devices used for video calling in addition to a good, working cell phone or landline. Another important factor in maintaining and managing your business is having all the appropriate forms for intake, exercises, and other tools. If you are managing your business in an outside environment, then the same applies in terms of equipment, but other risk management evaluations have to be implemented. For example, is the location safe and are you sharing the office with others? Do you need insurance, an alarm, and other safety measures like fire safety? Other things that you will need to evaluate are whether you can afford to hire other coaches or staff like an office manager to assist with paperwork and if you still need business appropriate credentials like legal entity credentials. Another aspect of your business is having the appropriate financial software or perhaps a CPA. You may want to consult with one prior to obtaining an LLC for your business, creating a business plan including a budget to ensure that your business will thrive financially, and also keeping accountability to the IRS and other information.

Knowing the laws of your county or state is important to ensure that you follow all guidelines required by the states. Knowing where you stand is important as you will need to make sure that your business grows, is kept organized, and has credibility in the business world. You want to make more money, but you also want to make sure that you have the capacity and manpower to deliver. Therefore, starting small and increasing is feasible as you are learning the ropes, and once your business has a stable foundation, you want to continue growing or expanding either with products you sell, clients, or earnings. Becoming educated in all of these areas will determine your success and if you can hire others to take on the task, then make sure that they are vested and committed to your mission as well as trustworthy.

Any expansions should be discussed with your CPA accountant to ensure that you have monetary support, capacity, and sustainability. Do you know how to create a budget? If not, start exploring any Excel or budgeting course that you can take to help you with the financial management of your business. The following questions will help you explore about maintaining and managing your business.

Questions

Maintaining and Managing

36. What payment apps are you familiar with? Do you know how to create a business plan? How familiar are you with creating and keeping a budget or business plan? Do you know how to create a website? Are you familiar with any platforms that offer websites? Have you met with a CPA? How open are you to obtain coaching from a business coach? What 3 goals would you like to achieve in this area?

_____

_____

_____

_____

_____

_____

_____

_____

_____

_____

_____

_____

_____

Conclusion

In Conclusion, when I began authoring this book, I wanted to share some of the things that I learned as trial and error when I began my journey of becoming a life coach and starting my business. In this journey, I learned that you would encounter many barriers, stagnation, and challenges due to a lack of resources and support or a lack of planning. Going back to the beginning, I searched for a good school to obtain my life coaching certification as opposed to a 30-day coaching program offered by many life coaches. These programs are great to start but if you want to receive a good foundation in life coaching and learn all the theoretical, application, and actual internship coaching sessions not only with other students but also with outside clients. Prior to enrolling in a 1-year program at Southwest Institute of Healing Arts in Tempe, Arizona, I took a 3-month program life coaching program with Steve Jones, which actually set the foundation for my life coaching journey; in addition to NLP certification, which allowed me to learn about body language, cognitive, behavioral responses. While this short training encompassed tons of great videos and homework, it was not as intense as a 1-year program. There are other great schools to choose from and many vary in price, it's up to you to choose the one that you can afford or the one that you feel will provide you with the best theoretical foundation in life coaching. Finally, when I was ready to start my business, I began first by creating a business plan with the tasks, actions, and resources needed. I also created my own vision board with exactly what I envisioned for my goals and business. I completed a vision and mission statement to help guide and keep me focused in the right direction. I also began to create all of my business forms, such as intake, client rights, agreements, and other tools. As I started to accomplish some of the tasks, I felt more confident that I was gearing towards the right path. I was getting the ball rolling by taking action steps in manifesting my new career and business. I read books, listened to videos, spoke with people, and also received coaching in this area for about 6 months before moving to Florida.

During this whole process of preparation, I continued working in the role of Sr. Director of Clinical Services for Permanent Supportive Housing. Working with my life coach, I set goals each month for my business and to stay on track. I continued to do a lot of research on my own, from how to design a website, get clients, and research other life coach websites and services. I continued to receive life coaching myself from 4 different coaches at different phases of my life. All of these coaches contributed to my progress, growth, and in developing my own life coaching style. They were all different with different specialties, but I got a lot of business coaching from some of them except the first, which was a little bit not so my style because her beliefs did not align with my morals and values. However, she was an amazing person and an excellent life coach, she did provide me with valuable insights during our coaching journey. I had to stop the coaching session although she was an amazing human being; it was not the type of coaching I needed. Like I tell my clients, you have to click with your coach, and it is not a clingy, friend zone click, but of mutual respect and connection based on what they bring to the table and how they help you discover the primary issues that you need to work on. Some of them became my mentors who briefly coached me in different areas that I needed coaching in.

As I began to complete some of my business goals, I realized that I needed a better logo and branding. Marketing and branding were something I could not do on my own, therefore, I met with a marketing coach who helped me explore and motivate me to create my own branding, refine my vision and mission statement. The results were amazing and personalized; my coach did an amazing job with my marketing and branding as well as my business cards. A good majority of the work in the journey I was able to complete but some that were more specialized and needed professional guidance to ensure that I use the right tools and manage finances accordingly required the support of a professional.

With this, I am saying that it is important to obtain outside help when needed to assist you in areas in which you lack experience. In my case, it was the finance aspect, social media, and branding. Once I achieved the knowledge and refined my expertise, I am now able to manage my business more effectively. In the very same way that you are working towards creating your platform as a life coach. It is advisable to obtain life coaching mentoring from other coaches in any areas that you feel may be hindering you from growth or that you feel that you still need to do more exploration, change, or growth. Let's say you are struggling with some of the financial aspects of the business, it is advisable to hire a business coach to help you set your business foundation and learn everything you need to manage your business effectively as well as to work on future sustainability. If you are weak in some areas of your life, for example, in organization or procrastination; you may want to hire a coach that is specialized in this area to help you become more organized and learn how to tackle procrastination. There are life coaches that help with self-image as well as any other areas you may feel that you need mentoring or support. This is why life coaching is such an amazing field as you will find many individuals with extensive knowledge and experiences on different topics of interest or services needed that help with empowering others.

Writing this book has not only been a dream come true for me, but it has allowed me to also refine some areas of my life, my business, and it has transformed me into wanting to be an excellent coach, mentor, and teacher for others who are seeking to start their own business in this area. I believe that you learn more and become better at what you do when you are helping others. And this book is a tool that I wished I had when I began my journey.

I pray that this book and guide can be instructional for all who read it, and may it provide you with a wealth of many different tools and ideas to explore that will help you stay motivated to continue to work on your dreams and goals.

Much love and blessings,

Claribel Coreano, MS. Transformational Life Coach
Empower Global Coaching

Quotes & Resources

1. Claribel Coreano, Original quote from page 13, 16,18, 21, 25, 26, 29, 36, 41
2. Seneca, page 41, quote retrieved from www.goodreads.com
3. Gregory Kent, page 41, retrieved from www.goodreads.com
4. Ashley Lorenzana, page 41 retrieved from www.azquotes.com
5. Deepak Chopra, page 60, retrieved from www.Iamfearlesssoul.com
6. Jeffrey McDonalds, page 60, retrieved from www.iamfearlesssoul.com
7. Roy T Bennett, page 61, retrieved from www.goodreads.com
8. Lauren DeEstafano, page 65, retrieved from www.brightdrops.com
9. Eddie Huang, page 69, retrieved from www.brainyquotes.com
10. G. Campbell Morgan, page 70, retrieved from www.christianquotes.com
11. E.M. Bounds, page 73, retrieved from www.christianquote.com
12. Anonymous, page 78, retrieved from www.awakenthegreatnesswithin.com
13. Abdul Kalam, page 83, retrieved from www.awakengreatnesswithin.com
14. Pooja Agnihotri, page 91, retrieved from www.goodreads.com
15. Pooja Agnihotri, page 101, retrieved from www.goodreads.com
16. Leo Tolstoy, page 105, retrieved from www.blog.hubspot.com
17. Dr. Masaru Emoto, page 106, retrieved from www.goodreads.com
18. John Laroche, page 111, retrieved from www.quotefancy.com

19. Tory Burch, page 119, retrieved from www.bigcommerce.com
20. Steve Maroboli, page 123, retrieved from www.goodsreads.com
21. Jim Rohn, page 127, retrieved from www.awakenthegreatnesswithin.com
22. Jeffrey R. Holland, page 128, retrieved from www.goodsreads.com
23. Ezra Taff Benson, page 132, retrieved from www.goodreads.com
24. Bob Proctor, page 135, retrieved from www.quotemaster.org
25. Melody Beattie, page 137, retrieved from www.brainyquotes.com
26. Frank A Clark, page 140, retrieved from www.brainyquote.com
27. Idowu Koyenikan, page 151, retrieved from www.goodreads.com
28. Rasheed Oguntaru, page 155, retrieved from www.goodreads.com
29. Dareen Hardy, page 164, retrieved from www.azquotes.com
30. Steve Jobs, page 166, retrieved from www.azquotes.com
31. James Altucher, page 167, retrieved from www.azquotes.com
32. Debbie Hampton, page 173, retrieved from www.quoteambition.com
33. James Altucher, page 181, retrieved from www.ezquotes.com
34. Steve Jobs, page 190, retrieved from www.snopes.com
35. Steve Jobs, page 190, retrieved from www.bloghubspot.com

References

Merriam Webster Dictionary, page 83 retrieved from **www.merriamwebsterdictionary.com**

Vine's Expository Dictionary of Old and New Testament Words ©1996, which copyright is now restored by the GATT Treaty to W.E. Vine Copyright, Ltd, Bath, England, page 984, word sacred, (page 124)

Index of Biblical Passage Cited

Scripture quotations in this publication appear from the following bible version: New King James Version. Copyrighted @1979, 1980, 1982 by Thomas Nelson, Inc, Publishers

Used by permission. All rights reserved.

The New King James Version of the Bible

The English Standard Version of the Bible

The New Living Translation Version of the Bible

1. Jeremiah 29:11 Page 8, 10
2. Romans 15:13 Page 20
3. John 16:33 Page 20
4. Philippians 4:13 page 31
5. Hebrews 11:1 page 44
6. Proverbs 3:5-6 page 48
7. Jeremiah 29:11 page 57
8. Psalm 27:14 page 69
9. Ecclesiastes 3:11 page 69
10. 1st Timothy 3:1 page 74
11. Nehemiah's 4:1-4 Page 74
12. Psalm 37:4 page 79

Resources/Tools

Here is a list of all the resources and tools that you will need as you embark in building your business. Many blessings, Claribel

Marketing

Software to manage your business:
http://www.clientcompass.com
http://www.Functionpoint.com
http://www.Kantata.com
http://www.Productive.com
http://www.Cooper.com
http://www.AgencyAnalytics.com
http://www.worksuite.com
http://www.mediatool.com

Programs to help fill your practice:
http://www.fillyourpractice.com
http://www.noomii.com
http://www.practice.com
http://www.coachaccountable.com
http://www.paperbell.com
http://www.nudgecoach.com

Directory website to list your coaching services:
http://www.greattherapists.com
http://www.noomii.com
http://www.coachfederation.org/need
http://www.barks.com

Coaching programs:
http://www.ipeccoaching.com

http://www.coachingfederation.com

http://www.certifiedlifecoachinstitute.com

http://www.coahing-online.org

http://www.lifepurposeinstitute.com

http://www.Erickson.edu

http://www.coachville.com

http://www.udemy.com

http://www.americanuniversityofNlP.com

http://www.southwestinstituteofhealingarts.com

Reasonable priced logos design:

http://www.gotlogos.com

http://www.canvas.com

http://www.adobeexpress.com

Inexpensive business cards and other marketing/promotional items:

http://www.vistaprints.com

http://www.canvas.com

http://www.staples.com

Become a credit card merchant:

http://www.practicespaysolution.com

Accept credit card payments with your mobile phone and/or tablet:

Square Credit Card Reader:

- IOS: http://store.apple.com/us/product/H8332LL/B/square-credit-card-reader
- Android: http://play.google.com/store/apps/details?id=com.squareup

Alternative methods of accepting payments:

- http://www.paypal.com

- http://www.quickbooks.com
- http://www.clover.com
- http://www.paysafe.com
- http://www.merchantone.com
- http://www.stripe.com

How to Start a Successful Coaching Business: 2024 Guide:
By Luisa Ahou/Coaching Business. http://www.luisazhou.com

The Ultimate Starting a Coaching Business Checklist (Super In Depth!) https://lovelyimpact.com

The Checklist You Need to Start a Coaching Business (by Sami Toussi, one of thousands of Career Coaches on Noomii. Article posted April 10, 2021. From http://www.noomii.com

6 Proven Steps to Scale Your Coaching Business Successfully by Shubham Sethi https://www.entrepreneur.com

Website Resources:
Find and Register Domain names:
- http://www.godaddy.com
- http://www.register.com
- http://www.netsol.com

Web Site Hosting/most come with Search engines links
- http://www.godaddy.com
- http://www.1and1.com
- http://www.euni.com
- http://www.wix.com
- http://www.squarespace.com
- http://www.wordpress.com

Emailing lists, auto responders and shopping cart/Website builder programs:

- http://www.cartville.com
- http://www.godaddy.com/hosting/website-builder.aspx?ci=76392
- http://wesite.1and1.com/?___reuse=1375467931358
- http://www.quickpaypro.com
- http://www.aweber.com
- http://www.getresponse.com

E-Newsletter Resources:

- http://www.wordpress.com
- http://www.constantcontact.com
- http://www.benchmark.com
- http://www.mailchimp.com
- http://www.convertkit
- http://www.omnisend.com

Help for creating an e-mail newsletter using WordPress:
http://www.wpbeginner.com/wp-tutorials/create-a-free-email-newsletter-service-using-wordpress/

Content for newsletter:

- http://www.topten.org
- http://www.beehiv.com
- http://www.bestcrucial.com
- http://www.academylike.com

e-Zine Directory to list your newsletter:
http://www.ezines.nettop20.com

Article Resources:
http://www.vretoolbar.com/articles/directories.php

EBOOK Resources

Turn your ebook into a PDF format

http://www.neevia.com

http://www.AllYouCanBooks.com

http://www.perlego.com

http://www.openlibrary.org

Create and Compile your e-book

- http://www.palmettoppublishing.com
- http://www.bookbaby.com
- http://www.canva.com
- http://www.ebookmaestro.com
- http://www.desktopauthor.com
- http://www.ebookscompiler.com

E-Books covers:

- http://www.killercovers.com
- http://www.canva.com
- http://www.delaney-designs.com
- http://www.pixelled.com

EBook directory to submit your ebook to:

http://www.ebooksubmit.com

https://e-booksdirectory.com

https://www.hotvsnot.com

Seller and publisher of e-books

http://www.booklocker.com

https://www.fronlinewriters.com

https://www.palmettopublishing.com

https://www.kdp.amazon.com.en_US

https://www.press.barnesandnoble.com

E-book publishing:
https://www.amazon.com/gp/seller-account/mm-summary-page.html?topic=200265020
https://www.palmettopublishing.com
https://www.danbrownacademy.com
https://www.kdp.amazon.com.en_US

Turn your ebook into a printed tips booklet
http://www.tipsbooklet.com
https://www.palmettopublishing.com
https://www.bookbaby.com
https://www.gorhamprinting.com
https://www.hongkiat.com

Turn your ebook into a book:
https://www.palmettopublishing.com
https://www.bookbaby.com
http://www.flippingbook.com
https://www.kdp.amazon.com.en_US

Book/Self-Publishers:
http://www.sherisesstudios.com/
http://www.apub.com
http://www.amazonprofs.com
https://press.barnesandnoble.com
https://www.palmettopublishing.com
https://guide.authorhouse.com
https://westbowpress.com
http://www.genesispublishinghouse.com/

Christian Book Publishers:
http://www.elmhillbooks.com/
http://www.tbnandtrilogychristianpublishing.com
http://www.kingdomselfpublishing.com

Speaking and Networking Resources:
http://www.toastmasters.org
http://thespeakerlab.com
http://www.linkedin.com
http://speakercoop.com

Speaker's Universities:
http://www.schrift.com
http://epichabit.com
http://ww.thebalancemoney.com

Resources for professional speakers:
https://nsaspeaker.org
http://www.speakernetnews.com
http://professional.dce.harvard.edu
http://speakerflow.com

National Speakers Association:
https://nsaspeaker.org
https://www.developgoodhabits.com

Free articles on Public Speaking:
http://www.public-speaking.org
https://hbr.org
https://www.nytimes.com/

Listing of Associations:
- http://www.uschamber.com
- http://www.rotary.org
- http://www.kiwanis.org
- https://directoryofassociations.com
- https://causeiq.com

Networking:
- http://www.letip.com

- http://www.bni.com
- https://www.investopedia.com
- https://www.betterup.com
- https://www.careereducaiton.columbi.edu
- https://hbr.org
- https://www.alignable.com/groups/brave-public-speaking-for-women-entrepreneurs

Facebook Private Networking Groups:
Women Helping Women Entrepreneurs
She-Rises Studios Community
Business Leaders Network
Professional Christian Coaching
Empowered Women
The Christian Life Coaching Network

Press Resources:
Free press release distribution services
http://www.Prweb.com
https://www.einpresswire.com
https://www.newsire.com
https://www.freelancer.com

PR Coaches:
http://www.publicityinsider.com
https://www.gloriachoupr.com
https://www.theprmastercoach.com

Get listed as an expert and receive emails from reporters looking for excerpts for stories.
- www.prnewswire.com/profnet/
- www.prleads.com
- https://blog-justreachout.io
- https://readdle.com

Starting your practice:
Free web course on how to start a business:
http://www.myownbusiness.org
https://www.swyftfillings.com
https://www.mailchimp.com
https://www.legalzoom.com
https://www.entrepreneur.com
https://www.scu.edu
https://www.edx.org

Business planning tool:
https://www.Netsuite.com
https://www.capterra.com
https://www.anaplan.com
http://www.businessplans.org

IRS Small Business and Self-Employed Tax Center:
http://www.irs.gov/Businesses/Small-Business-&Self-Employed

Small Business Administration guide to legally structure your coaching business:
http://www.sba.gov/catergory/navigation-structure/starting-managing-business/starting-business
To obtain your LLC you must apply to your local state government office. For example, for the state of Florida is sunbiz.com

Professional liability insurance:
- https://www.biberk.com
- https://www.aig.com
- https://www.thehartford.com
- http://www.geico.com
- http://www.insurancequotes.com
- http://www.ideafit.com/fitness-insurance/life-coach-insurance

- http://www.iac.lockton-ins.com/pl
- http://www.insurance-certifiedcoach.com

Training and Accreditation
- https://www.Udemy.com
- http://www.coachville.com
- https://www.fiacoaching.com
- https://www.nshcoa.com
- http://www.coachfederation.org
- http://www.certifiedcoach.org
- http://www.icf.com
- https://www.certfiedlifecoachinstitute.com

Other resources:
Set up online appointments:
https://www.capterra.com
https://www.appointment.briskcloudware.com
https://calendly.com
https://workspace.google.com
http://www.appointmentquest.com

Virtual Assistant/appointments setters:
https://www.viraltick.com/

Receive faxes on your computer:
http://www.efax.com
https://online-faxformswift.com
https://www.myfax.com
https://www.apps.microsoft.com

Podcasting:
https://www.bigvu.com
https://www.anchor.com
https://www.spotify.com

https://www.swell.com

Time management:
https://www.trello.com
https://www.clockify.me
https://www.friday.app

Connecting all social media:
https://www.linktree.com
https://www.getapp.com
https://www.socialconnect.com
https://www.crowdfire.com

Social media:
Instagram: https://instagram.com
Facebook: https://facebook.com
WhatsApp: https://Whatsapp.com
Tik Tok: https://tiktok.com
YouTube: https://Utube.com
Twitter: https://twitter.com

Internet security:
McAfee: https://www.mcafee.com
Norton: https://www.norton.com
Total Av: https://www.totalav.com
Surfshark: https://www.surfshark.com
NordVPN: https://www.nordvpn.com

OFFERING YOU THE TOOLS YOU NEED TO BE EQUIPPED FOR LIFE!

SO, YOU WANT TO BE A LIFE COACH?
Life Coaching Guide & Workbook

With Empower Global Coaching

Empower Global Coaching was founded by Claribel Coreano and officially opened for business in 2023. As part of my journey as a life coach, I saw the need to document and share my journey in a book. So, You Want to Be a Life Coach? was created and inspired by my own journey to becoming a life coach. When I started authoring this book, I did not know which way it was going to go. I wanted to share a little bit about my own journey but also provide the readers with some tools, resources, and practice to help guide them along the road to accomplishing their dreams of becoming a life coach. The Book shares inspirational quotes, motivation, and encouragement but also provides you with some critical thinking topics to engage you to proactively participate by answering some questions that will help you brainstorm on where you are in your journey, how to get started, tools you need, and lastly managing your business.

Empower Global Coaching offers

For more information, contact Info:

egc_2325@empowerglobalcoaching.com

We are always looking for individuals who are seeking life coaching opportunities, guest speakers for the "Be An Encourager" podcast, and trauma and dating coaching groups.

SEE WHAT WE DO

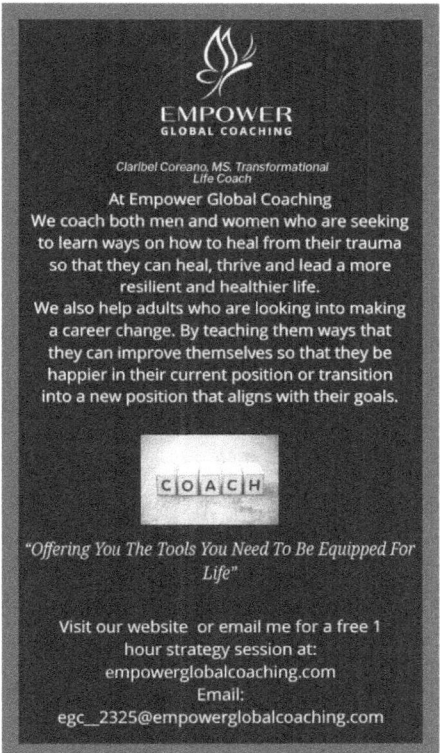

Podcast   Books   Services

About the Author

My name is Claribel Coreano. I am a Transformational Life Coach, writer, and artist. I am a native of the Dominican Republic, born in Santiago. I moved to New York City with my family at the age of eight years old, and we then relocated to Connecticut after six years of living in Manhattan, NYC. I received a Master's Degree in Human Services with a concentration on Marriage and Family Therapy and Psychology from Capella University, I completed several Life Coach certifications from the Southwest Institute of Healing Arts Tempe, Arizona in 2015. Additional certifications I have received include Certified Life Coaching NLP and Women's Empowerment Life Coaching. Before completing the Life Coaching Certification I worked in the social services field for over 27 years, working first with the HIV/Aids population. When I first began my career it was during the beginning of the epidemic, and after three years, I changed to working with the homeless population - those suffering from mental health issues, substance abuse, and other socioeconomic problems. I have worked with individuals, youths, veterans, and families. I raised four sons, one of whom has served the country in active war in Afghanistan and who is now a disabled Army veteran. My oldest is a coordinator for a health care agency, my third son is a licensed optical design and dispensing technician, and my youngest is a successful business owner and personal trainer.

On a personal level

In my spare time, I dedicate myself to my hobbies of writing and painting. I started painting in 2002 and progressively improved my skills. I consider myself an intuitive artist, and this is because I have not been professionally trained as a painter. Most of my paintings come from my imagination and with no training or knowledge of mixing colors and painting techniques. I have developed my own style by using different mediums of texture, paper, napkins, aluminum, gesso, and glue. For painting, I use knives, my fingers, Q-tips, pencils, needles, and of course brushes to achieve what I visualize in my mind. The final colors come gradually as I add them until they become the right color. Then, I know that it is completed. I am also more of an eclectic painter because I don't paint with only one style but focus on whatever I visualize in my imagination and then transfer it onto the canvas. Why do I paint? It helps me relax and visualize something beautiful then transfer it onto a canvas. Writing has always been a hobby of mine since I was young and I have written poetry, done journaling and wrote a poetry book in 2006 which I am working on revising. I currently have three manuscripts ready to be published.

My Experience and Expertise

Why did I want to become a coach? I wanted to help others who had experienced trauma, and domestic violence, who are single mothers raising children on their own. As a domestic violence and childhood trauma survivor, I have never considered myself a victim but always a survivor. I know firsthand what is needed to overcome obstacles, negative mindsets, trauma, and abuse. I learned how to defeat negative self-image, mindset, and trauma, all of which I was able to overcome with the help of counselors and life coaching. Resiliency has allowed me to overcome many hardships I have faced in my life. It has become my mission to help others build resiliency, become empowered, and gain self-esteem to help them live their best lives. My life has been a testament to the strength of the human spirit and the power of God's love, and I hope to inspire others who are facing similar difficulties. I experienced many difficulties throughout my life, but I am happy to say that throughout all these trials God provided me with the courage and hope that I needed. Life has not been easy for me; however, I gained a lot of wisdom from all of my experiences. I consider myself a truly fortunate individual. I am a survivor! As a result of all these experiences. I felt inspired to share what I have accomplished as a young mother experiencing domestic violence, raising my children, learning about relationships, and accepting everything as a lesson learned.

About my business:
Based in Spring Hill, Empower Global Coaching is a professional coaching service dedicated to helping individuals, groups, and companies achieve their personal and professional goals. I offer a wide range of coaching services including individual and group life coaching, spiritual coaching, and support groups for single individuals, marriage-focused individuals, parents, youths, and companies looking to build stronger teams. These sessions promote self-empowerment and will help you grow, expand, and heal. I will provide you with the guidance and support you need to make positive changes in your life and reach your full potential.

Mission:
We work with clients who are looking to heal from trauma and domestic violence improve their relationships, learn parenting skills, and health & wellness by establishing a positive coaching relationship that helps you to **CREATE THE LIFE YOU WANT TO LIVE and BE THE PERSON YOU WANT TO BECOME.**

Clients:
"I work with both (male/females) to create a more empowered life by coaching to produce transformational growth in their careers, relationships, families, health & wellness, and spirituality.

My approach:
I employ a client-centered transformational coaching approach and experience by accepting each person's individuality, circumstances, and

coaching needs. I seek to be a positive motivator of encouragement that will assist each individual in learning about themselves and their circumstances by exploring the areas where growth is needed.

Services
- Individual Coaching
- Women's Empowerment Coaching
- Relationship, Family, and Adolescent coaching
- Health & Wellness Coaching
- Spiritual Coaching
- Group coaching on healing trauma, dating, parenting skills, self-esteem, and confidence.

www.ingramcontent.com/pod-product-compliance
Lightning Source LLC
Chambersburg PA
CBHW070916120626
46546CB00001B/281